Life Hacks Unlocked

Awesome, Useful, Handy Tricks to Make Life Easier

Jett Thompson

Journey Together LTD

Copyright © 2025 by Journey Together LTD

All rights reserved.

No portion of this book may be reproduced in any form without written permission from the publisher or author, except as permitted by U.S. copyright law.

Contents

	Introduction Welcome to the Shortcut Society	1
1.	Time Hacks More Hours, Less Chaos	3
2.	Tech Hacks Tame Your Tech	11
3.	Home Hacks Your Home, Simplified	20
4.	Work Hacks Smarter, Not Harder	31
5.	Brain & Focus Hacks Mind Like a Ninja	38
6.	Travel & On-the-Go Hacks Move Like a Pro	49
7.	Health & Wellness Hacks Fit(ish), Happy, and Functioning	59
8.	Cures, Fixes & Quick Solutions Because You Don't Have Time to Google It	65
9.	Survival & Safety Hacks MacGyver Your Way Through It	76
10.	Money & Budget Hacks Save Without Suffering	83

Conclusion & Bonus Tips
"Your Shortcut Starter Pack"

Introduction

Welcome to the Shortcut Society

Let's be honest—life isn't getting simpler.

We're juggling more than ever: work, errands, apps, passwords, never-ending to-do lists, and that one drawer full of tangled cords and expired chargers. We're managing calendars, money, mental fatigue, forgotten laundry, and maybe a dozen browser tabs open—literally and mentally. It's no wonder that "getting through the day" often feels like a full-time job.

This book isn't for people with perfect routines and flawless systems. It's for the rest of us—the ones doing our best, living full lives, and trying not to burn out. The ones who don't want another complicated strategy... just a **smarter, easier way through the mess**.

The Shortcut Society is about working with reality, not against it. It's about finding the fastest path to calm, clarity, or "done enough." These hacks don't ask you to be more disciplined or squeeze more into your day. They help you simplify, smooth things out, and move forward with less friction.

Inside these pages, you'll find **more than 500 clever hacks**—some practical, some surprising, some that might just blow your mind. There are smart systems for time, focus, tech, and home. There are travel tricks that make airports less awful, and money hacks that help you spend smarter without spreadsheets. There are **focus tools for scattered brains**, **digital cleanups**, **mental resets**, and **household shortcuts** that feel like cheating (in a good way).

But this book also goes further.

Because sometimes life doesn't just need streamlining—it needs rescuing.

That's where the **survival hacks** come in. The ones for when you're running on fumes, when your bag breaks in the rain, and when you need a fix and you need it fast. These aren't abstract ideas—they're real, gritty, *how-to-hold-it-together* tools that make everyday chaos survivable.

And then there are the **cures, fixes, and tricks** you never knew you needed. How to stop a zipper from sticking. How to make your pillow supportive again. What to do when your shoes smell, your throat burns, or your internet dies before a call. The kinds of solutions most people would Google—if they had the time. Now? You've got them all in one place.

TIt could bea manual for productivity. It's a field guide for functioning.

Flip to the chapter you need most. Or read it straight through. Everything's short, practical, and low-effort—designed to work whether you've got five minutes or just enough energy to try one thing today.

Because in the end, this isn't about doing more. It's about finding clarity, energy, and relief in the middle of real life.

You're not scattered. You're overloaded.

You don't need a full reset. You just need a few better shortcuts.

So if you're ready to stop Googling your way through every daily mess...Welcome to the Shortcut Society.

Let's dive in.

First stop: Time Hacks – More Hours, Less Chaos.

Time Hacks

More Hours, Less Chaos

Time is the one thing we never seem to have enough of. Between work, errands, family, and everyday life, it's easy to feel like you're constantly behind. But what if you could reclaim little pockets of time—not by doing more, but by doing things smarter?

This chapter is filled with simple tricks to help you cut through the noise, stay focused, and get things done without the stress. From time-blocking to micro-habits, these hacks are designed to bring a little more ease and a lot more clarity to your day.

The 2-Minute Rule: Because Procrastination Hates a Running Start

You know those little tasks that nag at you all day? The email you need to send, the bill you have to pay, and the overflowing junk drawer that mocks you every time you look at it? If it takes less than 2 minutes, just do it. Right now.

Sure, it sounds almost too simple. But the magic of the 2-Minute Rule is that it gets you started. And once you start, momentum takes over. That email turns into an empty inbox. The paid bill becomes a balanced budget. The junk drawer sparks a full-on decluttering spree. All because you took 120 seconds to get the ball rolling.

- **Hack #1:** The 120-Second Solution

See a tiny task, do the tiny task—right then and there. Those 2-minute to-dos add up to major momentum (and way less nagging).

- **and Hack #2:** The One-Thing Win

Before diving into your day, ask yourself: What's one small task I can knock out right now to start the day right? Then do it. Victory breeds victory.

- **Hack #3:** The Post-It Prompt

Stick a note that says "Could this be done in 2 minutes?" somewhere you'll see it often. It's a friendly little reminder to just get it done.

Time-Blocking Without the Burnout: Your Calendar Is Your Friend

Raise your hand if this sounds familiar: You start your day with a vague idea of what needs to get done, but before you know it, it's 3 PM and you're wondering where the time went. Enter time-blocking, the gentle art of making your calendar work for you, not against you.

Here's how it works: Divide your day into chunks of time, and assign each chunk a specific task or type of task. It could be 45 minutes for focused work, followed by 15 minutes for email and messages, then another focused block, then a break to stretch and refuel. Repeat until quitting time.

- **Hack #4:** The Time Chunk System

Divide your day into focused blocks—45 minutes of deep work, 15 minutes for email. Repeat. Realistic planning means more doing, less drifting.

- **Hack #5:** The Task Sandwich Method

Sandwiching a tricky task between two easier ones. Knock out something simple to start, then ride that momentum through the tougher job. Finish with another quick win.

- **Hack #6:** The Ebb-and-Flow Schedule

Make your time blocks match your energy levels. Tackle tougher tasks when you're at your peak, and save easier stuff for those afternoon slump hours.

- **Hack #7:** The Theme Day Trick

Assign certain days of the week to recurring types of work, like "Meeting Mondays" or "Focus Fridays." It reduces decision fatigue and helps you mentally gear up for what's coming.

- **Hack #8:** The Buffer Block Builder

Add 15-minute buffers before and after meetings or major tasks. It gives you breathing room, prevents time crashes, and makes you feel like you're ahead of your schedule, even when you're not.

- **Hack #9:** The No-Meeting Zone

Block out at least one hour a day on your calendar for "Deep Work Only." Defend it like it's sacred. You'll be shocked how productive you become with just one protected hour.

The ABCDE Method: A Cheat Code for Your To-Do List

Quick show of hands: Who here has a to-do list that's longer than a grocery receipt on a hungry day? We've all been there. But what if there was a way to cut through the clutter and focus on what really matters? Enter the ABCDE Method.

Here's how it works: Take your sprawling to-do list and give each item a letter grade. "A" tasks are urgent and important—the things that will have serious consequences if you don't do them ASAP. "B" tasks are important but not urgent—they'll move the needle, but the world won't end if they wait till tomorrow. "C" tasks would be nice to do, but aren't essential. "D" tasks can be delegated. And "E" tasks can be eliminated altogether.

- **Hack #10:** Grade Your Tasks from A to E

"A" tasks are urgent and important. "E" tasks can be eliminated. Do the A's first and the E's never. Goodbye, to-do list overwhelm.

- **Hack #11:** The Top Three Techniques

Circle the three tasks that absolutely must happen today to feel like you've won the day. Do those first, no matter what. Everything else is gravy.

- **Hack #12:** The Monthly Must-Dos

At the start of each month, make a list of 5-7 bigger-picture items that you need to tackle that month. Check it weekly to make sure you're chipping away at those key goals.

- **Hack #13:** Task Triaging Before Bed

Each night, scan tomorrow's list and assign ABCDE ratings. You'll sleep better knowing what really matters—and wake up with a plan, not panic.

- **Hack #14:** The "D for Delegate" Dump

Create a running list of tasks that you could delegate. Whether it's to a colleague, your partner, a VA, or an app—getting those "D" tasks off your list frees up mental bandwidth.

- **Hack #15:** Eliminate Like a Boss

Be ruthless with the "E" category. Ask: "If I never do this, will anyone notice?" If not, ditch it. Clearing clutter isn't just for closets—it's for calendars too.

Batching: The Secret to Smoother, More Productive Days

Picture this: It's Monday morning, and you're feeling fresh and ready to tackle the week. You sit down at your desk, fire up your computer, and... promptly spend the next hour flitting between your inbox, your project list, and that funny cat video your coworker sent you. Sound familiar? Welcome to the club.

But what if there was a way to cut through the noise and get more done in less time? Enter batching, the art of grouping similar tasks together and tackling them all at once.

- **Hack #16:** Bring Like With Like

Group similar tasks and tackle them in one fell swoop. Replying to emails? Do 'em all at once. Errands? Knock 'em out back-to-back. Smoother days, right this way.

- **Hack #17:** The Context Clumping Method

Clump tasks by the "mode" they require: creative work, busywork, calls and meetings, errands. Letting your brain stay in a groove saves time and mental energy.

- **Hack #18:** The Weekly Batch Prep

Pick a time each week (Sunday nights, maybe) to batch prep for the week ahead: pack lunches, pick outfits, etc. It's like a gift to your future self.

- **Hack #19:** Calendar Color Coding

Assign colors to different types of batched tasks: Admin, Creative, Personal, Errands. Visually, it helps your week feel more intentional—and makes overload easier to spot.

- **Hack #20:** Morning Power Hour

Designate one hour in the morning to batch your biggest recurring tasks. The rest of the day will feel lighter, and you'll already be ahead by 9 a.m.

- **Hack #21:** The Inbox Sweep

Check email just 2–3 times per day in one focused block. The rest of the time? Shut it down. Most "urgent" messages can wait at least an hour.

Tech Tools for Time Tracking: Because Every Minute Counts

Let's face it: Time has a way of slipping away from us, no matter how good our intentions. But what if there was a way to keep tabs on those elusive minutes and hours, without adding another item to your already-packed to-do list? Enter time tracking tools, the ultimate accountability buddies for your busy day.

Here's the deal: There are a ton of apps and programs out there designed to help you track your time, from simple timers to full-fledged project management systems. Some are free, some come with a price tag, but all of them have one thing in common: They make it easy to see exactly where your time is going, so you can make better choices about how to spend it.

- **Hack #22:** The Automatic Time Tracker

Try RescueTime or Timely—they run in the background, secretly spying on your digital day. Prepare for surprising insights into where your minutes go.

- **Hack #23:** The Pomodoro Timer Twist

Use a Pomodoro timer app (like Focus Timer or Pomodoro Technique) to work in focused 25-minute bursts with 5-minute breaks. Highly effective for powering through procrastination.

- **Hack #24:** The Pen-and-Paper Reality Check

Go analog and just jot down start and end times for your tasks. Sometimes the simplest method is all you need to spot those sneaky time sucks.

- **Hack #25:** Screen Time Smackdown

Check your phone's screen time dashboard at the end of the day. It's a truth bomb—but the first step to reclaiming hours you didn't know you were losing.

- **Hack #26:** The Time Audit Challenge

For one week, log everything you do in 30-minute blocks. You don't have to do it forever, but it's an eye-opener that reveals leaks you can fix.

- **Hack #27:** The "Zero-Based" Time Budget

Just like a zero-based budget, assign every hour of your day a purpose—even if it's rest or play. When time has a name, it's less likely to vanish.

Setting Invisible Boundaries: The Art of Saying "Not Now"

Picture this: You're in the middle of focused work, making serious progress on that big project. Suddenly, your phone buzzes with a notification. It's not urgent, but it's distracting enough to pull you out of your flow. Sound familiar?

In a world where we're constantly connected, it can feel like we're at the mercy of every ping, ding, and ring. But what if there was a way to take back control of our time and attention, without having to go completely off the grid? Enter invisible boundaries, the art of saying "not now" to the things that don't serve us.

- **Hack #28:** The VIP Notification System

Go to phone settings. Turn off notifications for everything except your VIP contacts and crucial apps. Ahhh, listen to that focus. Feels good, right?

- **Hack #29:** The Email Empty-Out

Set up email filters to sort incoming messages into "Urgent," "Semi-Urgent," and "Non-Urgent" folders. Empty that Urgent box first, then chip away at the rest when you've got spare focus.

- **Hack #30:** The Deadline Defense

Put your project deadlines in your shared calendars and use them as a polite deflection for less-urgent requests. A gentle "Can't this week, but maybe next!" works wonders.

- **Hack #31:** The Silent Mode Strategy

Turn your phone on silent (not vibrate!) during deep work. No buzz, no ding, no distraction. Tell close contacts they can call twice if it's urgent.

- **Hack #32:** Office Hours—At Home

If you work from home or have kids around, set visible "office hours" using a sign, calendar, or color cue. It trains others to respect your time—and reminds you to protect it too.

- **Hack #33:** The "Ask Me Later" Note

Keep a shared doc or whiteboard where people can jot down non-urgent requests for you to review when you're done with your current block. It reduces interruptions without ignoring people.

BONUS MICRO-HACKS (Quick Hits Worth Mentioning)

- **Hack #34:** Default Calendar Settings – Set new meetings to default to 25 or 50 minutes. Everyone appreciates the buffer.

- **Hack #35:** "Closed Tabs Only" Rule – No new browser tabs during focus time. If it's not urgent, it can wait.

- **Hack #36:** The One-Touch Rule – If you open it (email, letter, app), handle it. Don't just read and leave it for later.

- **Hack #37:** "No-Scroll Zones" – Designate times of the day (first hour after waking, last before sleep) as scroll-free zones.

- **Hack #38:** The Sunday Reset – Take 30 minutes every Sunday to plan the week ahead. It saves hours of decision-making and aimless drifting.

Tech Hacks

Tame Your Tech

Technology should make life easier—but let's be honest, sometimes it just adds to the chaos. Between endless apps, constant notifications, and a growing list of digital clutter, it's easy to feel overwhelmed by the very tools meant to help you.

This chapter helps you take back control. With smarter shortcuts, app pairings, and quick digital cleanups, you'll streamline your tech and make it work for you, not the other way around.

Best Apps for Productivity and Sanity

Ever open your phone and feel instantly overwhelmed by pages of apps you haven't touched in months? That clutter isn't just digital—it's mental too. Every extra swipe and scroll eats away at your time and attention.

That's where the Three-App Rule comes in. Highlight the three apps that genuinely help you—like a calendar, a note-taking app, or a wellness tracker—and give them VIP status on your home screen. The rest? Tuck them into folders, hide them, long-press what no longer serves you.

- **Hack #39:** The Home Screen Reset

Delete everything from your home screen, then add back only what you use daily. Prioritize your top 3 apps and tuck the rest into folders.

- **Hack #40:** The Weekly App Audit

Check your screen time every Sunday. Ask: What added value? What stole my focus? Keep the good, cut the rest.

- **Hack #41:** The Notification Purge

Turn off all non-essential notifications. If it doesn't help you, it doesn't need your attention.

- **Hack #42:** Thee

Group apps by function—Work, Health, Finance, etc. Organizing makes finding and ignoring them easier.

- **Hack #43:** The App Hideaway

Move time-wasting apps to a separate screen or hide them entirely. Out of sight, out of scroll.

App Pairings That Actually Work

Some apps are solid on their own, but when you pair them up, they become your digital dream team. Whether it's Forest plus Spotify for focus, or a task manager synced to your calendar, these combos amplify your flow and cut down the friction.

One underrated duo? A password manager and a scanning app. Together, they turn random paper clutter into organized, secure digital files you can access in seconds. Think smarter, not harder.

- **Hack #44:** The Focus Combo

Pair your music app with a focus timer like Forest. Boosts flow, reduces distraction.

- **Hack #45:** The Calendar Sync-Up

Connect your calendar and task manager. Automate reminders and block time for top priorities.

- **Hack #46:** The Paper Killer

Scan key documents with apps like Adobe Scan. Save them to cloud folders linked with your password manager.

- **Hack #47:** The Routine Launcher

Use apps like Shortcuts (iOS) or Tasker (Android) to automate routines like bedtime, workouts, or writing.

- **Hack #48:** The Cloud Stack

Stack apps like Notion + Google Drive + Zapier to create custom workflows for recurring tasks.

Hidden Phone Features That Save Time

Tired of typing the same things over and over—your email address, your home address, or that perfectly worded "per my last email"? Good news: your phone can do the heavy lifting for you.

Both iPhone and Android have a **text replacement** feature that lets you turn a few characters into full phrases. For example, ";em" can auto-expand to your email address, or ";mtg" to "I'm running a few minutes late—be there soon!" It's like having a tiny assistant in your pocket, minus the judgment and the salary.

- **Hack #49:** The Email Shortcut

Create text shortcuts for frequent phrases. ";em" = your email, ";mtg" = meeting template.

- **Hack #50:** The Swipe Sprint

Swipe typing is faster than tapping. Try it for a day and watch your texts fly.

- **Hack #51:** The Cursor Trick

Press and hold the spacebar to turn your keyboard into a trackpad. Move your cursor precisely.

- **Hack #52:** The One-Hand Wonder

Switch to one-handed mode on your keyboard when multitasking.

- **Hack #53:** The Hidden Menu

Long-press on app icons to reveal hidden shortcuts. Great for jumping straight to tasks.

Password Manager + Master Trick

Your phone's full of secret weapons you probably aren't using. From text replacements that finish your sentences to gesture-based controls that make you feel like a tech ninja, these hidden features can save you loads of time.

Start with the basics: shortcuts for your email and address, swipe typing, spacebar cursor control, and one-handed modes. Once you unlock these, even everyday typing becomes faster and smoother.

- **Hack #54:** The Password Purge

Use Bitwarden or 1Password to store and autofill passwords. Replace weak ones as you go.

- **Hack #55:** The Master Formula

Create a sentence you can remember, then convert it to a strong master password with numbers and symbols.

- **Hack #56:** The Family Vault

Set up shared vaults for family accounts—banking, bills, subscriptions.

- **Hack #57:** The Autofill Win

Enable autofill in your browser and apps to save precious seconds on logins.

- **Hack #58:** The Security Check

Run your password manager's security audit to clean up reused and outdated logins.

Two-Factor Everything (Without the Headache)

Two-factor authentication (2FA) might sound like a hassle, but it's one of the easiest ways to protect your accounts. Start with your most important ones—email, banking, anything with payment info—and work your way down.

Use apps like Authy instead of SMS for more secure codes, and save backup options in your password manager. It takes minutes to set up, but it can save you hours of stress if anything goes wrong.

- **Hack #59:** The Authenticator Upgrade

Use Authy instead of SMS for two-factor authentication. Safer, and you won't get locked out.

- **Hack #60:** The Priority Protection

Start with your email, then secure your financial accounts. Email is the gateway to everything.

- **Hack #61:** The Code Backup

Store recovery codes in your password manager or print them out and lock them up.

- **Hack #62:** The Multi-Device Sync

Choose apps that sync 2FA codes across your devices, like Authy.

- **Hack #63:** The Recovery Net

Add secondary recovery options: backup phone numbers, alternate emails, and trusted contacts.

Email Zero: Stop Drowning in Inbox

Your inbox shouldn't be in charge of your time. Turn off notifications and set two or three dedicated times a day to check emails—no more constant tab switching or reacting to pings. When you do open it, stick to the one-touch rule: reply, archive, delete, or task it. No rereading. No clutter.

Make it even easier on yourself by setting up filters for important contacts, unsubscribing from anything you no longer read, and creating a few quick-response templates for messages you send often. With a few tweaks, your inbox becomes a tool again, not a time trap.

- **Hack #64:** The Scheduled Inbox

Only check emails at set times—10 am, 1 pm, 4 pm. Turn off all notifications.

- **Hack #65:** The One-Touch Rule

When you open an email, act: reply, task it, archive it, or delete it. No re-reading.

- **Hack #66:** The Unsubscribe Sprint

Unsubscribe from 10 newsletters today. Use tools like Unroll.me to speed up the purge.

- **Hack #67:** The VIP Filter

Create filters so only priority emails (boss, spouse, clients) reach your inbox immediately.

- **Hack #68:** The Template Toolkit

Create go-to templates for thank-yous, follow-ups, and polite declines.

Screenshot Shortcuts & Screen Recorders

Why type out a wall of instructions when a quick screenshot or screen recording can do the job better and faster? Your devices already have these tools built in, and using them can save you (and everyone else) serious time and frustration.

Need to walk someone through a step-by-step? Just record it once and send it off. Want to point something out clearly? Snap it, circle it, label it. Whether you're solving tech problems or sharing how-tos, visuals make communication sharper and simpler.

- **Hack #69:** The Annotated Screenshot

Snip + circle + send. Use markup tools to highlight what matters.

- **Hack #70:** The Troubleshooting Show

Record a short video showing the issue instead of explaining in long texts.

- **Hack #71:** The Visual Tutorial

Need to show someone a step-by-step? Record your screen once, send it forever.

- **Hack #72:** The Quick Access Key

On Windows, press Win+Shift+S. On Mac, Command+Shift+4. Practice it.

- **Hack #73:** The Mobile Recorder

Enable screen recording on your phone for sharing demos or app issues.

Document-to-Done Pipeline

When you stumble on something important—an idea, an instruction, a task—don't just leave the tab open and hope you'll remember. Instead, capture it. Screenshot the key info, clip it with a web tool, or send it straight to your notes or task manager.

This small shift turns fleeting moments into organized action. No more digging through old emails or scrolling through tabs. From spark to follow-through, your ideas now have a place to go—and a plan to get done.

- **Hack #74:** The Action Snapshot

Screenshot key info and send it to your task manager with a due date.

- **Hack #75:** The Digital Commonplace

Keep a folder of saved screenshots of quotes, notes, or ideas that inspire action.

- **Hack #76:** The Tab Killer

Instead of keeping 30 tabs open, screenshot the info and close the tab. Your RAM will thank you.

- **Hack #77:** The Email Extract

Screenshot key parts of important emails and drop them into your notes app to reference.

- **Hack #78:** The Clipper Combo

Use web clippers in Evernote, Notion, or OneNote to pull important snippets with one click.

Organize Your Files So You Actually Find Stuff

Your digital files don't have to be a mess. A simple naming format—like YYYY-MProject_DocumentType—can bring instant order and make searching a breeze. Combine that with a weekly cleanup of your Downloads folder, and you'll always know where things are.

Pick one cloud service to store everything important, then use built-in tools like batch renaming and system search shortcuts to stay organized. A tidy digital workspace means fewer headaches and way less time spent hunting for "final-final-final2.docx."

- **Hack #79:** The Naming Convention

Use YYYY-MM-DD_Project_DocumentType naming for every file. Sorts clean, looks smart.

- **Hack #80:** The Weekly File Sweep

Each Friday, clean your Downloads folder and Desktop. 10 minutes max.

- **Hack #81:** The Batch Rename

Rename entire groups of files at once using built-in OS tools.

- **Hack #82:** The Search Pro

On Mac, use Spotlight (Cmd+Space). On Windows, tap the Windows key and search by keyword.

- **Hack #83:** The Cloud Cleanout

Choose one cloud platform. Move everything there and remove duplicates from others.

The Digital Declutter

Digital clutter sneaks up on you—downloads, screenshots, duplicate files, old projects. Just like with your closet, it piles up fast. A simple monthly reminder to clear out the junk, archive what's worth keeping, and free up space goes a long way.

Use tools to find duplicates, wipe unnecessary screenshots, and check what's hogging storage. It's not flashy, but this low-effort habit keeps your tech running fast—and your brain feeling a little lighter.

- **Hack #84:** The Monthly Cleanup

Put a 30-minute cleanup on your calendar every month. Stick to it.

- **Hack #85:** The Storage Map

Use apps like DaisyDisk or WinDirStat to find what's hogging space fast.

- **Hack #86:** The Archive Folder

Create one catch-all "Archive" folder for files you want to keep but rarely need.

- **Hack #87:** The Duplicate Destroyer

Use a duplicate finder tool monthly to get rid of digital clutter.

- **Hack #88:** The Screenshot Sweep

Every two weeks, delete screenshots you no longer need. They pile up fast.

Home Hacks

Your Home, Simplified

Your home doesn't need to be perfect to feel peaceful. In fact, small, consistent habits often make the biggest difference. Whether you're dealing with clutter, endless laundry, or meal-planning burnout, there's a simpler way.

This chapter is packed with quick wins and smart shortcuts to bring more calm, flow, and function into your home. Because when your space feels better, so does everything else.

5-Minute Tidy-Up System

Mess happens. Life's busy, and your home shouldn't have to be spotless to feel calm. But a quick reset can do wonders. Enter the 5-minute tidy-up—a fast, focused way to reset a room (or two) without losing your evening.

Pick a timer, blast some music, and give yourself just five minutes. Focus on surfaces, visible clutter, or anything out of place. You'll be amazed at how much better everything feels with a little intentional chaos control.

- **Hack #89:** The Reset Timer

Set a timer for 5 minutes and tidy one space—keys on hooks, dishes in the sink, stuff off the floor. Done.

- **Hack #90:** The Basket Sweep

Grab a laundry basket and do a fast walk-through, collecting anything that's out of place. Rehome after.

- **Hack #91:** One-Room Rule

Before bed, pick just one room to reset. Bonus points if it's the one you wake up in.

- **Hack #92:** Power Playlist Pick-Up

Create a 5-minute playlist for cleaning bursts. When the song ends, so does the tidy-up.

- **Hack #93:** The 3-Item Fix

When you walk into a room, put away or fix three things. It's effortless—but adds up fast.

- **Hack #94:** Family Flash Clean

Call a 5-minute cleaning blitz with the whole household. Set a timer and go. Kids love the race.

Lazy Consistency is key

Meal planning sounds great in theory—until you're staring at a blank calendar and wondering what on earth to make next Tuesday. The fix? Don't overcomplicate it. Think in themes, keep a rotating list of go-to meals, and simplify.

You're not building a Pinterest-perfect menu. You're feeding people. The goal is less stress, less waste, and a plan that actually works. Even a loose plan beats daily guesswork.

- **Hack #95:** Theme Nights

Assign easy categories: Pasta Monday, Taco Tuesday, Sheet Pan Wednesday. It narrows the choices.

- **Hack #96:** The Meal Matrix

Create a 3x3 grid of proteins, veggies, and starches. Mix and match for endless combos.

- **Hack #97:** Prep, Don't Cook

Wash and chop produce in advance. Future you will be forever grateful.

- **Hack #98:** One Master List

Keep a list of 10 go-to meals your family loves. Rotate them weekly with small twists.

- **Hack #99:** Double It Up

When making a freezer-friendly meal, double the batch. One for now, one for later.

- **Hack #100:** Lazy Lunch Kit

Create grab-and-go bins in your fridge for lunches: one with proteins, one with fruits, one with snacks.

- **Hack #101:** The "No-Cook" Night

Designate one night for sandwiches, cereal, or leftovers. It's a break with zero guilt.

Fridge Organization That Cuts Waste

The average household wastes over $1,500 in food yearly, and a messy fridge is often to blame. When food gets lost, it gets tossed. But with a little structure, your fridge can go from a black hole to a well-oiled machine.

Use bins, zones, and clear containers to keep things visible and accessible. Label leftovers, rotate items weekly, and treat your fridge like real estate: prime space goes to what gets used most. A little visibility goes a long way when it comes to saving money and reducing waste.

- **Hack #102:** The Fridge First Zone

Create a "use this first" bin for aging produce, leftovers, or opened items.

- **Hack #103:** Shelf by Type

Assign each shelf a job—snacks, meals, condiments, drinks. It helps everyone in the house find things (and put them back).

- **Hack #104:** Clear Containers Only

Use see-through bins and boxes so you can actually see what you have.

- **Hack #105:** Label + Dat, It

Write the date on opened leftovers or sauces. It prevents mystery meals.

- **Hack #106:** Sunday Fridge Reset

Pick one day a week to clean out and take inventory. Plan meals from what's inside.

- **Hack #107:** Egg Carton Hack

Flip an empty egg carton upside down to create a riser. Instantly add a second layer of storage.

- **Hack #108:** Snack Zone for Kids

Designate a low shelf for kid-approved snacks. Gives them independence and saves you time.

Command Center for Chaos Control

A family calendar on the fridge isn't a plan—it's a sticky, half-forgotten hope. You need a true command center: one place where the whole household knows what's happening, what's needed, and what's next.

Consistency is key, whether it's a chalkboard wall, a corkboard, or a digital dashboard. Keep it in a visible, central spot. Use it daily. And keep it simple enough to actually maintain it. The less complicated it is, the more likely you'll actually stick with it.

- **Hack #109:** The Visual Hub

Set up a space with a calendar, shopping list, and chore chart—all in one glance.

- **Hack #110:** One-Pager Rule

Everything fits on one sheet. No binders. No chaos. Just the essentials.

- **Hack #111:** Color Coding System

Assign a color to each family member for events, tasks, and appointments.

- **Hack #112:** The Daily Reset Check

Before bed, glance at the command center. Prep backpacks, keys, and anything for tomorrow.

- **Hack #113:** The Inbox Basket

Place a bin for incoming papers, forms, and receipts. Process weekly. Clutter, contained.

- **Hack #114:** The Weekly Sync-Up

Do a 10-minute Sunday night huddle to walk through the week ahead.

Everyday Items with Surprising Uses

Your house is full of hidden superheroes—ordinary things with unexpected powers. You don't always need a specialty cleaner, tool, or gadget. Sometimes the best solution is already sitting in your cabinet.

A toothbrush becomes a detail scrubber. Toothpaste fixes scuffed shoes. Coffee filters clean screens. Welcome to the surprisingly brilliant side of home hacks. It's not about having more stuff—it's about using what you already have in smarter ways.

- **Hack #115:** Toothpaste Polish

Use white, non-gel toothpaste to buff scuffs off shoes and sneakers.

- **Hack #116:** Coffee Filter Screen Cleaner

Wipe TV and phone screens with a dry coffee filter. No lint, no scratches.

- **Hack #117:** Binder Clip Cable Catcher

Clip them to the edge of your desk to hold charging cables in place.

- **Hack #118:** Towel Roll Drawer Divider

Roll hand towels or washcloths to separate items in messy drawers.

- **Hack #119:** Rubber Band Jar Opener

Wrap a rubber band around stuck lids for instant grip and twist power.

- **Hack #120:** Ice Cube Gum Remover

Press an ice cube on gum stuck in fabric or carpet. Freeze, scrape, done.

Decluttering by Zones, Not Rooms

Trying to declutter a whole room can be overwhelming. The trick? Break it down by zone, not size. Instead of "tackle the living room," try "clear the coffee table," or "clean out the TV cabinet."

Small wins stack up quickly. And when you focus on function (not square footage), it's easier to maintain long-term. Decluttering gets way more doable when your goal is one drawer, not an entire room.

- **Hack #121:** 20-Minute Zone Clean

Pick one small area and set a timer. Toss, keep, donate—no overthinking.

- **Hack #122:** The Drop Zone Check

Clean up the area where clutter always gathers: the entry table, kitchen counter, or your desk.

- **Hack #123:** Function-First Sorting

Sort items based on use: daily, weekly, or rarely. Store accordingly.

- **Hack #124:** Visible Surface Rule

Clear and wipe one visible surface each day. It sets the tone for the whole room.

- **Hack #125:** One-In, One-Out

Every time something new comes in (shoes, mugs, toys), something old goes out.

- **Hack #126:** The Hidden Hotspots

Declutter drawers, under beds, and cabinet backs. The stuff you never see? It adds up.

Low-Maintenance Plant Parenting

You don't need a green thumb—or a jungle-worthy windowsill—to bring life into your home. Even a single healthy plant can make a space feel more vibrant, fresh, and calming. The secret? Pick the right plants, give them a decent spot, and keep your care routine simple.

Hardy houseplants like snake plants or pothos don't demand much attention, but they still give you all the aesthetic and mood-boosting perks. Keep them near indirect light, set a consistent watering schedule, and stop stressing about perfection. The goal isn't to create an indoor greenhouse—it's to add beauty without adding burden.

- **Hack #127:** The Three-Plant Starter Pack

Start with a snake plant, pothos, and ZZ plant—three low-maintenance indoor legends that thrive in low light, don't need daily watering, and still look amazing.

- **Hack #128:** Watering Day Reminder

Pick one watering day per week. Set a recurring phone reminder. Done.

- **Hack #129:** The Drainage Check

No drainage = root rot. Add pebbles to the bottom of non-draining pots to give roots a fighting chance.

- **Hack #130:** Bright But Not Direct

Place plants near windows, but out of harsh direct sunlight. Most indoor plants love filtered light.

- **Hack #131:** The Finger Test

Stick your finger an inch into the soil—if it's dry, it's time to water. No fancy tools needed.

- **Hack #132:** Leaf Wipe Refresh

Dust collects on leaves. Wipe them gently with a damp cloth once a month for that fresh, healthy look.

Cleaning Hacks That Feel Like Cheating

Cleaning doesn't have to mean hours of scrubbing and sweating. With a few smart tricks, you can get high-impact results in a fraction of the time. The goal is to work smarter, not harder, letting tools and timing do the heavy lifting.

Focus on high-traffic areas, build small routines into your day, and make cleaning less about the grind and more about smart shortcuts. A little effort here and there can create a home that feels fresh, without draining your entire weekend.

- **Hack #133:** The Steam Shower Shine

After a hot shower, spray down your bathroom surfaces. The steam does half the scrubbing for you.

- **Hack #134:** Dishwasher Everything

Run toys, sponge holders, toothbrush caps, pet bowls, and even flip-flops through the dishwasher (top rack only!).

- **Hack #135:** Overnight Oven Spray

Spray oven cleaner at night, close the door, and wipe it out in the morning. No elbow grease needed.

- **Hack #136:** The Sock Mop Trick

Put an old sock over a Swiffer or broom to dust hard-to-reach places like blinds and baseboards.

- **Hack #137:** The One-Bucket Method

Carry a small caddy of supplies from room to room. You'll clean faster with everything in reach.

- **Hack #138:** Wipe + Walk Away

Spray counters or stovetops, let the cleaner sit for 5 minutes, then wipe. Give your product time to shine.

Maximize Small Spaces

Living small doesn't mean living cluttered. Whether it's a studio apartment or a tight guest room, a few clever tweaks can make a space feel bigger, brighter, and more functional.

It's all about making every inch count. Think vertical storage, multi-use furniture, and hiding everyday items in plain sight. Living in a small space gets a lot easier when your stuff has a place and your layout has a purpose.

- **Hack #139:** The Over-Door Hero

Use over-the-door racks for shoes, cleaning supplies, or pantry goods. Hidden storage, instantly.

- **Hack #140:** The Fold-and-Tuck

Keep foldable baskets, stools, or tables that you can tuck away when not in use.

- **Hack #141:** Under-the-Bed Goldmine

Use storage bins, bags, or drawers under your bed for seasonal clothes, extra linens, or shoes.

- **Hack #142:** Wall Hooks Everywhere

Add wall hooks in closets, hallways, or behind doors. Great for coats, hats, or bags.

- **Hack #143:** Furniture with Storage

Choose ottomans, benches, or coffee tables that double as storage. Sneaky, stylish, and smart.

- **Hack #144:** The Shelf Stretch

Add shelves higher on the wall to draw the eye up and create more usable vertical space.

Laundry That Doesn't Pile Up (Much)

Laundry never really ends, but it doesn't have to run your life either. A few smart systems can make it manageable, even automatic. The key? Build small habits, delegate where possible, and simplify the process.

No more "clean but still in the basket" piles. From sorting to folding, small tweaks can streamline the cycle and keep things under control, even in the busiest households.

- **Hack #145:** The Load-a-Day Rule

Do one load per day, start to finish—wash, dry, fold, put away. It prevents laundry mountains.

- **Hack #146:** One Hamper Per Person

Give each family member their own hamper. No sorting required—just wash and return.

- **Hack #147:** The Fold Station

Set up a small table or space near your laundry area with a basket for each person. Fold straight from the dryer.

- **Hack #148:** Dryer Sheet Drawer Freshener

Toss a dryer sheet into your drawer or closet to keep clothes smelling fresh between washes.

- **Hack #149:** Sock Bag System

Use mesh bags for socks—one per person. Wash them together, there will be no more mismatched pairs.

- **Hack #150:** Clean Laundry Hang Zone

Hang a rod over your laundry area to immediately hang-dry delicates or wrinkle-prone items.

Reset Your Bedroom for Better Rest

Your bedroom should help you recharge, not remind you of what you haven't finished. Creating a restful space doesn't mean a full makeover.

A few intentional tweaks can make your bedroom feel like a sanctuary again.

Think less clutter, softer lighting, and better bedtime routines. When your space supports your sleep, everything else in life starts to feel more manageable.

- **Hack #151:** Nightstand Reset

Keep only the essentials: a lamp, water, and maybe a book. Clear the rest.

- **Hack #152:** The Bed-Making Habit

It takes 90 seconds and instantly makes the room feel cleaner. Do it first thing.

- **Hack #153:** Light-Level Control

Use warm bulbs, dimmers, or bedside lamps to shift your room's energy from busy to calm.

- **Hack #154:** Under-Bed Bin for Bedtime Stuff

Store extra blankets, books, or slippers under the bed in a lidded bin.

- **Hack #155:** No-Charge Zone

Keep your phone off the nightstand. Try charging it across the room—or outside the bedroom altogether.

- **Hack #156:** Sunday Sheet Swap

Pick one day a week to change your sheets. Fresh linens = instant upgrade to your sleep space.

Work Hacks

Smarter, Not Harder

Whether you're in an office, working from home, freelancing, or juggling meetings from your car, work doesn't have to feel like a grind. The right tweaks—tiny, simple, smart—can save you hours, stress, and sanity. This chapter is all about making your workday feel lighter, faster, and more focused.

We're not here to glamorize hustle culture. Instead, we're clearing the digital and mental clutter and making space for deeper focus and smarter workflows. From trimming meeting madness to cutting inbox chaos, these hacks help you reclaim control of your time and energy.

The Best-Kept Keyboard Shortcuts

If your hands are on the keyboard, keep them there. Keyboard shortcuts are the unsung productivity heroes—small but mighty. Learning just a handful can help you get more done, faster, without the constant click-fest between tabs, windows, and menus.

Start with your most-used tools: email, browser, documents, and calendar. The learning curve is small. The time savings? Huge. Once you start using them, there's no going back.

- **Hack #157:** The Copy-Paste Pro

Learn Ctrl+C, Ctrl+V, Ctrl+Z, Ctrl+Shift+V. That last one pastes without formatting—clean magic.

- **Hack #158:** Tab Tamer

Use Ctrl+Tab to flip between open browser tabs. Ctrl+Shift+T reopens that tab you just accidentally closed.

- **Hack #159:** Screenshot Shortcuts

Print Screen, Cmd+Shift+4, or Win+Shift+S—know how to capture your screen fast. It's perfect for sharing bugs, ideas, or receipts.

- **Hack #160:** Search Anything

Hit Ctrl+F (or Cmd+F) to find what you need instantly in emails, docs, or long articles. No scrolling necessary.

- **Hack #161:** Quick Window Toggle

Alt+Tab (Windows) or Cmd+Tab (Mac) lets you swap apps instantly. Useful when multitasking like a boss.

- **Hack #162:** Calendar Shortcut Keys

In Google Calendar? Hit "D" for day view, "W" for week, and "C" to create an event. Because yes, time blocking can be fast too.

How to Stop Being CC'd to Death

CC: the tiny inbox terror that multiplies by the minute. One second you're sipping your coffee, and the next, your inbox is 37 messages deep, with 35 of them saying "Thanks!" or "Noted." Sound familiar?

Here's the solution: set inbox filters, lead by example, and help your team stop auto-CCing everyone. It's about reducing email noise so you can focus on the stuff that actually needs your attention. The goal isn't to shut out communication—it's to make room for the messages that truly matter.

- **Hack #163:** The Filter Fortress

Create a rule for all emails where you're only CC'd. Label them "FYI" and move them out of your main inbox.

- **Hack #164:** The "Reply Smart" Move

Unless you're adding value, don't hit Reply All. If you're just observing, observe quietly.

- **Hack #165:** The Opt-Out Email

If you're getting looped into irrelevant chains, kindly ask: "Feel free to remove me from updates unless action is needed."

- **Hack #166:** The Shared Notes Trick

Move long email updates to a shared doc. Add highlights weekly. Everyone's updated, inbox spared.

- **Hack #167:** The Subject Line Standard

Encourage subject lines like "FYI," "Action Needed," or "Deadline Inside." It helps filter the chaos fast.

- **Hack #168:** The Office Hours Reminder

Let coworkers know when you're offline or unavailable. It reduces mid-meeting CC madness.

One-Minute Briefs for Meetings

Meetings are meant to move things forward, not drain hours from your day. Yet, too often, they feel aimless or bloated. The fix? Clarity. And it starts before you even hit "Join."

A one-minute brief forces everyone to focus: What's the goal? What are we deciding? Who truly needs to be there? This simple shift can make meetings faster, sharper, and—dare we say—useful. When people know what to expect, they show up more prepared, more focused, and far less frustrated.

- **Hack #169:** The Pre-Meeting Email

Send a short agenda in advance. It gives people a head start—and sometimes replaces the meeting entirely.

- **Hack #170:** The One-Pager Rule

Keep meeting notes on a single page. Bullet points only. If it doesn't fit, it's not essential.

- **Hack #171:** The Wrap + Recap

End every meeting with one minute of clarity: "Here's what we decided, here's what's next."

- **Hack #172:** Invite Less, Share More

Keep meetings small. Send a summary to others who just need the info, not the calendar block.

- **Hack #173:** The 15-Minute Cap

Challenge yourself to wrap it up in 15. Shorter meetings force clarity and focus.

- **Hack #174:** The "Do We Even Need This?" Test

If a Slack message or shared doc could do the job, skip the meeting. Protect everyone's time.

Fast Focus Reset (The 5-4-3-2-1 Trick)

Your brain wasn't built for constant task-switching. When you find yourself frazzled, unfocused, or spiraling through open tabs, you need a reset—and fast.

The 5-4-3-2-1 method is a grounding trick that brings your senses back to the present. In less than a minute, you shift from overwhelm to clarity. It's surprisingly effective—and always within reach. Think of it as a quick mental reboot when you're running low on focus fuel.

- **Hack #175:** Reset Ritual

When you feel scattered, pause and do 5-4-3-2-1. Close your eyes after if it helps.

- **Hack #176:** Screen Break Stretches

Pair the focus reset with a shoulder roll or wrist stretch. Your body (and brain) will thank you.

- **Hack #177:** The Distraction Tracker

Keep a sticky note where you jot down what pulls you off track. Reviewing it later reveals patterns and opportunities to improve.

- **Hack #178:** The Tab Tidy

When you refocus, close every tab except what you actually need. Less noise, more flow.

- **Hack #179:** Pomodoro Reset

Do a 25-minute focus sprint using a Pomodoro timer. When the buzzer hits, rest guilt-free.

- **Hack #180:** Nature Hit

Look out the window. Step outside. Even 60 seconds of greenery can calm your brain.

Declutter Your Digital Workspace

Your digital space should feel like a well-organized desk, not a chaotic junk drawer of half-named files and mystery screenshots. Digital clutter may be invisible, but it still adds stress and slows you down.

The good news? You don't need a total system overhaul. Just a few simple changes to how you name, store, and clean out your files can bring instant calm and control. And once you've felt the relief of a clean desktop, you'll wonder how you ever worked any other way.

- **Hack #181:** Desktop Zero

Clear your desktop at the end of each day. Drag everything into a folder if you must. Clean start tomorrow.

- **Hack #182:** Smart Folder System

Use broad categories like Finance, Projects, and Personal. Keep it simple, or you won't use it.

- **Hack #183:** Rename Like a Pro

Use this format: YYYY-MM-DD_Project_Keyword. Your future self will thank you.

- **Hack #184:** Cloud Sync Cleanse

Choose one platform (Google Drive, Dropbox, etc.) and stick with it. Chaos multiplies with each new app.

- **Hack #185:** Tool Audit

List every digital tool you use. Highlight the ones you actually need. Cut the rest.

- **Hack #186:** Tab-free Tuesdays

Once a week, close every open tab and start fresh. It's a digital deep breath.

How to Say "No" Without Guilt

Boundaries aren't rude—they're necessary. The ability to say no is one of the most powerful skills in your work life. But for many of us, it's also one of the hardest.

You don't need to explain yourself. You just need a kind, confident script—and the clarity to know when saying no is actually saying yes to your own priorities. A well-placed no protects your time, your energy, and your peace of mind

- **Hack #187:** The Soft No.

"Thanks so much for thinking of me—unfortunately, I can't take this on right now." That's it. No apology necessary.

- **Hack #188:** The Delay Deflector

Buy time by saying, "Let me check my schedule and get back to you." Gives you space to decide without pressure.

- **Hack #189:** The Redirect Response

Can't help? Suggest someone who might be a better fit. Keeps relationships strong while holding your boundary.

- **Hack #190:** The "Yes, But" Limit

Say yes—with conditions: "Yes, I can help if it's under two hours," or "Yes, but not until next week."

- **Hack #191:** Calendar Says No

Use your schedule as your scapegoat: "I'd love to, but I'm booked during that time."

- **Hack #192:** The Priority Check

Ask: "Is this aligned with my goals right now?" If not, that's your answer. No guilt required.

Brain & Focus Hacks

Mind Like a Ninja

Your brain is your best tool—but also your biggest distraction. Between pings, meetings, social media, and sheer exhaustion, it's no wonder focus feels slippery. This chapter is about getting your mind back on your side.

We're not here to push unrealistic productivity hacks. These are grounded, accessible tools you can grab when your attention starts drifting. Whether you're managing ADHD, mental overload, or just trying to concentrate for more than 12 minutes at a time, these hacks help you sharpen focus, reduce noise, and protect your brainpower.

Dopamine Fasts

Your brain loves a good hit of dopamine. That's the chemical rush you get from checking notifications, grabbing a snack, or scrolling TikTok. It's also what makes it hard to focus when you're constantly chasing the next hit.

A dopamine fast isn't about cutting out all pleasure. It's about giving your brain a break from overstimulation. Think of it as quieting the noise so you can hear your thoughts again. Even a short break can help reset your attention span and boost your ability to stay present.

- **Hack #193:** The 30-Minute Digital Detox

Pick one time each day to go completely screen-free. Let your brain breathe.

- **Hack #194:** Low-Stim Morning

Start your day without social media, emails, or news for the first 30 minutes. Give your mind a calm runway.

- **Hack #195:** The Notification Lockdown

Turn off all non-essential alerts. Every buzz is a break in your concentration.

- **Hack #196:** One Tab Challenge

Only keep one browser tab open at a time while working. Multitasking is a lie.

- **Hack #197:** Midweek Scroll Pause

Designate one day per week (like Wednesday) as your no-scroll day. Try books, walks, or journaling instead.

- **Hack #198:** Post-Project Wind Down

After big tasks, rest your brain. Sit quietly, go outside, or do something analog. Let your mind reset.

Pomodoro Twist: 25/5/15 Rhythm

You've probably heard of the Pomodoro method: 25 minutes of focus, 5 minutes break. But let's level it up. The 25/5/15 rhythm adds a longer break every fourth cycle to recharge deeper and avoid burnout.

It's not just about grinding—it's about pacing. With structured bursts and recovery, you can stay in the zone longer, without frying your brain. Think of it as interval training for your mind—focused sprints, followed by just enough rest to go again.

- **Hack #199:** Classic Pomodoro Core

Set a timer: 25 minutes work, 5 minutes break. Rinse and repeat for three cycles.

- **Hack #200:** The Deep Rest Block

Every fourth round, take a 15-minute break. Step away from screens and move your body.

- **Hack #201:** Focus Playlist Stack

Create playlists that match your Pomodoro blocks—25-minute songs or ambient loops.

- **Hack #202:** Task Chunk Mapping

Break your to-do list into Pomodoro-sized chunks. Each task = one block.

- **Hack #203:** The Buddy Sprint

Pair with a friend or coworker and work in sync, Pomodoro rounds. Accountability helps.

- **Hack #204:** The Pomodoro Journal

Track how many rounds you complete in a day and how you feel after each. Adjust accordingly.

Soundscapes That Improve Focus

Sound has a sneaky impact on your ability to focus. Too quiet? Your brain fills the silence with thoughts. Too loud? Instant distraction. But the right soundscape can guide your brain into a focused flow.

From lo-fi beats to nature sounds, soundscapes create an audio boundary around your focus time. It's less about blocking noise and more about replacing it with something purposeful. Think of it as background music for your brain—tuning out the chaos and tuning in to the task.

- **Hack #205:** Lo-Fi Power Hour

Use lo-fi beats or soft instrumental playlists to create a calm, focused zone.

- **Hack #206:** Nature Loop Boost

Rain sounds, waves, forest ambiance—nature loops lower stress and support deep work.

- **Hack #207:** Brainwave Entrainment

Try binaural beats or isochronic tones. Some frequencies sync with your brain's focus rhythms.

- **Hack #208:** White Noise Wall

Block external distractions with white noise. Ideal for open offices or noisy homes.

- **Hack #209:** The Audio Trigger

Use the same playlist or sound every time you work. Your brain starts associating it with focus.

- **Hack #210:** Silence as a Tool

Sometimes the best soundtrack is none. Use earplugs or noise-canceling headphones for pure silence.

How to Mentally "Bookmark" Ideas

You know that brilliant idea you had in the shower? Or that insight that popped into your head while driving, but disappeared before you could write it down? That's where mental bookmarking comes in.

Instead of trying to remember everything later, these hacks help you "tag" thoughts in the moment and capture them before they vanish. Because your brain is great at generating ideas, but not always great at holding onto them.

- **Hack #211:** The Word Anchor

Create a trigger word that brings the idea back. Example: "Greenlight" = presentation idea.

- **Hack #212:** Memory Pocket Notes

Keep a small notepad or notes app ready to capture ideas. Jot now, organize later.

- **Hack #213:** Physical Cue Placement

Move an object slightly out of place as a reminder. Keys on the floor = don't forget to follow up.

- **Hack #214:** Voice Memo Magic

Record quick voice notes as soon as the idea hits. Even one sentence is enough.

- **Hack #215:** Mind Map Replay

Mentally replay your day like a highlight reel at night. Capture anything worth keeping.

- **Hack #216:** Shower Sheet Hack

Use waterproof notepads in the shower to jot down thoughts. Yes, they exist—and they're genius.

Quick Visual Memory Tricks

Your brain is wired for images. That's why we remember faces better than names, or why visual learners thrive with diagrams. Use that to your advantage.

These simple visual hacks help you recall ideas, facts, or details faster by tapping into how your brain naturally works. It's not about memorizing harder—it's about making things more memorable. With the right visual cues, you can turn fleeting thoughts into sticky knowledge that actually sticks.

- **Hack #217:** The Color-Code Shortcut

Assign colors to categories (blue for finance, green for health, red for urgent). Your brain loves patterns.

- **Hack #218:** Picture the Page

When studying or reviewing, visualize the layout. Picture where the info was on the page.

- **Hack #219:** The Sticky Note Wall

Write ideas or tasks on individual sticky notes. Seeing them physically helps with recall.

- **Hack #220:** The Memory Walk

Associate each idea with a place in your home or a familiar route. A classic memory palace.

- **Hack #221:** Icon Cues

Use small drawings or emojis when taking notes. Simple icons boost retention.

- **Hack #222:** Snapshot Summary

Sketch a quick visual of what you learned or need to remember. Doesn't need to be pretty—just clear.

ADHD-Friendly Hacks for Staying on Track

Focus is a moving target, especially if your brain doesn't like sitting still. If you live with ADHD (diagnosed or undiagnosed), you know that productivity looks different. That's not a weakness—it's a different system that needs different tools.

These hacks are built for brains that bounce. They're fast, flexible, and forgiving. The goal isn't perfection—it's momentum. With the right structure and a little grace, progress is not only possible—it's sustainable.

- **Hack #223:** Microtask Magic

Break tasks into ridiculously small steps. "Open laptop" counts. Progress is progress.

- **Hack #224:** Time Blindness Busters

Use visual timers or time-tracking apps to stay aware of how long things actually take.

- **Hack #225:** Body Double Boost

Work beside someone else (even virtually). Their presence helps you stay anchored.

- **Hack #226:** Gamify the Grind

Turn tasks into mini challenges: "How much can I clean in 10 minutes?" Reward yourself.

- **Hack #227:** Change of Scene

If you're stuck, move. New environment = fresh energy. Try a café, a park, or just another room.

- **Hack #228:** The Restart Ritual

When you drift off task, don't spiral. Have a reset ritual—deep breath, stand up, pick one task, start again.

Mental Clutter Cleanup

Your brain holds many ideas, worries, reminders, tasks, and conversations. But when too much is floating around at once, it's like having 47 tabs open with music playing from somewhere. Cue mental overload.

These hacks are designed to help you clear the mental fog and feel lighter. Less noise in your head = more room for focus, creativity, and calm.

- **Hack #229:** Brain Dump Session

Once a day, write down everything on your mind—tasks, worries, random thoughts. No filter. Get it out so your brain can breathe.

- **Hack #230:** Morning Clarity Page

Start the day by answering three questions: What's one thing I must do? What can wait? What's already handled?

- **Hack #231:** Thought Parking Lot

Keep a running list (digital or paper) for ideas or distractions that pop up during focused work. You'll get back to them later with less stress.

- **Hack #232:** The One-Tab Mindset

Pick one task, one tool, and one tab. Everything else goes on pause until that's done. Simplicity sharpens focus.

- **Hack #233:** Weekly Worry Review

Block 10 minutes each Friday to review your biggest worries from the week. Cross off the ones that resolved themselves.

- **Hack #234:** Brain Detox Walk

Take a short walk—no phone, no podcast, just thoughts. Let your mind wander and settle on its own.

Note-Taking That Works for Your Brain

Taking notes isn't just about writing things down—it's about capturing and organizing info in a way your brain actually understands. The right note-taking system reduces stress, supports memory, and keeps you mentally organized.

Whether you're a doodler, bullet-pointer, or voice memo fan, these hacks will help you find a note-taking rhythm that sticks. Because when your notes work the way your brain works, everything feels just a little bit easier.

- **Hack #235:** The 3-Box Page

Divide each page into three sections: Key Ideas, Action Items, and Questions. Simple, clear, and repeatable.

- **Hack #236:** The 60-Second Recap

After every meeting, call, or class, take one minute to jot a recap. It helps lock in what matters.

- **Hack #237:** Visual + Verbal Combo

Add arrows, boxes, or doodles alongside your notes. Pairing visuals with text improves recall.

- **Hack #238:** Voice Note Vault

Too tired to type? Record quick voice memos and label them clearly. Great for on-the-go thinking.

- **Hack #239:** Digital Tag System

Use tags (like #projectX or #followup) in your notes app so you can quickly search and organize later.

- **Hack #240:** Sticky Summary

Write the one key idea from your notes on a sticky note and post it somewhere visible. It reinforces retention daily.

Decision-Making Under Pressure

Decision fatigue is real, and it drains your mental energy fast. When every little choice feels heavy, your focus disappears. But with the right tools, you can make better, faster decisions and protect your brainpower for the stuff that matters.

These hacks help cut through overthinking and get you into action. Because clarity isn't just a luxury—it's a focus-saver.

- **Hack #241:** The 10-10-10 Rule

Ask: How will I feel about this in 10 minutes? 10 days? 10 months? It helps break short-term fog.

- **Hack #242:** Binary Choice Method

Limit decisions to two clear options. It's easier to choose between A or B than A through Z.

- **Hack #243:** "Good Enough" Filter

If it's a low-stakes choice, stop at good enough. Not every decision needs to be optimal—just functional.

- **Hack #244:** Micro-Decide

When overwhelmed, just decide on the next step. Not the whole thing. One move at a time.

- **Hack #245:** The Sticky List Trick

Write three top priorities on a sticky note. If it doesn't fit on the note, it doesn't make today's cut.

- **Hack #246:** Externalize the Spin

Talk through your choices with a friend or a voice note. Sometimes saying it out loud brings instant clarity.

Energy Management for Your Brain

Focus isn't just about mindset—it's about managing your mental energy You're not a machine. You have peaks, dips, and cycles that affect how well your brain functions.

These hacks help you tune in to your energy levels and work with them, not against them. When you align your tasks with your energy, everything feels more doable—and less draining.

- **Hack #247:** Peak Time Power Block

Figure out when you're mentally sharpest (morning, afternoon, evening) and schedule important tasks then.

- **Hack #248:** The Energy Check-In

Before you start working, ask: Am I feeling focused, tired, wired, or scattered? Then adjust your plan to match.

- **Hack #249:** Recovery Microbreaks

Every 90 minutes, take a 5–10 minute reset—no screens, no scrolling. Breathe, move, reset.

- **Hack #250:** Task Rotation Rhythm

Alternate between high-focus and low-effort tasks throughout the day to preserve mental stamina.

- **Hack #251:** The "Battery Bar" Analogy

Visualize your energy like a phone battery. Top it up with rest, hydration, movement, and food before you hit zero.

- **Hack #252:** Light Reset Hack

If you're dragging mid-afternoon, get some natural light. Step outside, or sit by a window. Light = alertness.

Focus Triggers & Anchors

Focus doesn't always happen naturally, but it can be cued. With a few reliable rituals or sensory triggers, you can train your brain to drop into focus faster and more consistently.

Think of these like mental anchors. You use them regularly, and your brain learns: "Oh, it's time to get into gear." The more consistent the trigger, the stronger the response, like muscle memory, but for your attention span.

- **Hack #253:** The Focus Candle

Light the same scented candle every time you work. Your brain starts linking the scent to deep focus.

- **Hack #254:** Wear-to-Focus Mode

Have a designated "focus hoodie" or cap. It's your work uniform, even if it's just symbolic.

- **Hack #255:** The Countdown Ritual

Count backward from 5 and jump into the task. It gives your brain a cue to stop stalling.

- **Hack #256:** Entry Song Trigger

Play the same 30-second intro song before deep work. It signals "now we start" in your brain.

- **Hack #257:** Workspace Reset Cue

Clean or arrange your space before you begin. It tells your brain: we're switching modes now.

- **Hack #258:** Single-Task Switch Signal

Say out loud, "Now I'm working on X." It may sound silly, but declaring your focus helps reinforce it.

Travel & On-the-Go Hacks

Move Like a Pro

Travel is exciting—but let's be honest, it can also be chaotic. From packing stress to jet lag to lost chargers, even the smoothest trip has its share of friction. But a few clever tweaks? Total game-changers.

This chapter is your shortcut to stress-free travel. Whether you're hopping on a plane, heading out on a road trip, or just navigating a packed day, these hacks are here to help you stay organized, light, and ready for anything. You don't need to be a seasoned globetrotter to move like a pro—you just need a few tricks up your (carry-on) sleeve.

The goal: more freedom, fewer headaches, and a whole lot less scrambling.

One-Bag Packing Guide

Overpacking is a trap. Lugging around half your closet just means more stuff to lose, fold and carry. One-bag packing isn't just for minimalists—it's for anyone who wants freedom without the baggage.

The trick is to pick multipurpose clothes, pack in layers, and use compression cubes like a pro. Think: fewer "just in case" items, more "I actually wear this." Your shoulders—and your sanity—will thank you.

- **Hack #259:** The Rule of Three

Three tops, three bottoms, three pairs of underwear. Mix and match, then repeat.

- **Hack #260:** The Rolling Technique

Roll your clothes to save space and prevent wrinkles. Stack by outfit for extra ease.

- **Hack #261:** The Packing Cube Stack

Group clothes by category in cubes—tops, bottoms, undies, extras. It's like drawers for your bag.

- **Hack #262:** The Wear-on-Flight Layering

Wear your bulkiest items on the plane—sweaters, jackets, sneakers. Save space in your bag.

- **Hack #263:** Mini Laundry Kit

Pack a travel-sized detergent sheet and a sink stopper. Boom—instant laundry station.

- **Hack #264:** One Neutral Color Scheme

Stick to one color palette so everything matches. Bonus: you'll look effortlessly put-together.

Hotel Room Organization Tricks

Your hotel room isn't just a place to sleep—it's your temporary home base. A little order makes a big difference.

Instead of living out of your suitcase, create a quick setup system: shoes by the door, chargers in one spot, toiletries by the sink, snacks in the corner. You'll feel more settled and less like a human tornado passed through. A few minutes of setup can save hours of rummaging, stress, and forgotten items later.

- **Hack #265:** The Charger Hub

Designate one table as the charging zone. Plug in everything there—no more cord hunts.

- **Hack #266:** Shoe Bag Barrier

Put a small laundry bag or plastic shopping bag by the door for shoes. Keeps dirt contained.

- **Hack #267:** Towel Tray Trick

Lay a hand towel on the bathroom counter to corral toiletries. Mess stays minimal.

- **Hack #268:** The Quick Unpack

Use drawers or shelves for essentials. You'll feel grounded—and stop losing your socks.

- **Hack #269:** Hanger Hacks

Clip hotel hangers together with a rubber band or hair tie to hang more outfits without slipping.

- **Hack #270:** Snack Station Setup

Clear a corner or surface for your snacks, water, and vitamins. One spot = less rummaging.

Apps for Language, Money & Location

Your phone is your ultimate travel tool—if you load it with the right apps. From navigating new cities to handling currency to not butchering the local language, these apps do the heavy lifting so you can explore with confidence.

You don't need to download 20 apps. Just pick a few that cover your key needs, and you're good to go. The goal isn't tech overload—it's smart support that works offline, in transit, and when you're too tired to figure it all out.

- **Hack #271:** Language Lifesaver

Use Google Translate with offline languages downloaded. The camera scan feature? Pure magic.

- **Hack #272:** The Currency Converter

Install XE or a similar app to convert prices fast and avoid tourist tax traps.

- **Hack #273:** Offline Maps

Download Google Maps areas before your trip. No data? No problem.

- **Hack #274:** Local Ride + Transit Apps

Skip taxis. Use apps like Moovit, Uber, Bolt, or the local go-to to navigate like a local.

- **Hack #275:** ATM Locator Tools

Apps like Revolut or Wise show where to withdraw cash with the best rates (and lowest fees).

- **Hack #276:** The Phrasebook Shortcut

Bookmark key phrases or create flashcards in Notes. Practice in downtime—hotel to airport = study hall.

Avoiding Jet Lag (Sleep, Light & Hydration)

Jet lag is real—and brutal. It messes with your body clock, mood, and productivity. But a few smart moves can help you bounce back faster.

The big three: sleep, light, and hydration. Adjust your schedule before you fly, get daylight at your destination, and drink water like it's your job. Small shifts, big difference. Think of it as training your body to adjust like a traveler, not just a passenger.

- **Hack #277:** Pre-Flight Adjustment

Shift your sleep by 30–60 minutes a few days before travel. Easier landing ahead.

- **Hack #278:** The Light Trick

Expose yourself to bright light when it's morning at your destination—even if it's 3 AM for you.

- **Hack #279:** Power Nap Cap

Keep naps under 30 minutes to avoid grogginess. Use an eye mask to block distractions.

- **Hack #280:** Hydration Hustle

Drink water every hour in-flight. Skip alcohol and limit caffeine if possible.

- **Hack #281:** Compression Socks + Walks

Keep circulation moving to fight fatigue and stiffness. Walk the aisle. Flex those toes.

- **Hack #282:** The Arrival Routine

Land, shower, unpack, and eat a real meal—even if you're tired. Trick your body into adapting.

How to Make Airport Time Productive

Airports are weird limbo zones—lots of time, not much control. But with the right mindset, you can turn that wait into a win.

Whether it's getting work done, clearing your inbox, journaling, or catching up on podcasts, airport time can be reclaimed with a little intention. It's not about being hyper-productive—it's about turning downtime into something that feels useful, calm, or even a little creative.

- **Hack #283:** Offline Content Prep

Download books, shows, or podcasts before you leave. Airport Wi-Fi is a trap.

- **Hack #284:** The Email Cleanup Sprint

No better time to unsubscribe from junk mail than when you're waiting at Gate 14.

- **Hack #285:** Plan + Reflect Session

Use downtime to map your week, set goals, or review your trip notes. Brain dump = peace of mind.

- **Hack #286:** The Zone-Out Kit

Noise-cancelling headphones + eye mask = instant bubble. Great for recharging in public.

- **Hack #287:** Mini Body Reset

Stretch, walk laps, hydrate. Better than slouching in a chair, scrolling aimlessly.

- **Hack #288:** Creative Catch-Up

Use a note app to brainstorm, write, or sketch. Something about travel sparks ideas.

Snack & Toiletry Hacks for Your Carry-On

Your carry-on is prime real estate. Pack it right, and you'll avoid overpriced airport snacks, dry skin, and mid-flight chaos.

The best approach? Think comfort, fuel, and mini fixes for common travel annoyances. A few well-packed items can turn a cramped flight into something almost... enjoyable.

- **Hack #289:** Bento Box Snacks

Pack a small container with nuts, protein bars, fruit slices, and gum. TSA-friendly and better than airport food.

- **Hack #290:** TSA-Ready Toiletries

Pre-pack a clear pouch with solid versions of essentials—bar shampoo, toothpaste tabs, lotion sticks.

- **Hack #291:** Hydration Boosters

Add electrolyte packets or coconut water powder to your bottle. Keeps you hydrated on the go.

- **Hack #292:** Skin Rescue Kit

Include lip balm, hand cream, face mist, and a soothing balm. Airplane air is no joke.

- **Hack #293:** The Toothbrush Trick

A toothbrush and mini paste in your carry-on can reset your whole mood after a long flight.

- **Hack #294:** Sleep Survival Set

Eye mask, earplugs, and a neck pillow that doesn't suck. Sleep makes all the difference.

Clean & Fresh on the Go

Just because you're traveling doesn't mean you have to feel like a crumpled hoodie with airplane breath. With a few clever tricks, you can stay fresh, clean, and human—even without a proper shower.

These low-effort hygiene hacks are lifesavers for long layovers, road trips, or anywhere running water is scarce. A little prep = a lot of comfort. You don't need a spa day—you just need the right essentials in arm's reach.

- **Hack #295:** Wipe & Refresh Kit

Pack facial wipes, body wipes, and mini deodorant. Instant reset in airport bathrooms or rest stops.

- **Hack #296:** Dry Shampoo Lifeline

Bring a travel-size dry shampoo or powder. Greasy hair, handled in seconds.

- **Hack #297:** Pocket Laundry

Bring a few detergent sheets and a large ziplock. Wash essentials in a sink, hang dry overnight.

- **Hack #298:** The Flip-Flop Fix

Always pack a pair of lightweight flip-flops. Great for hotel showers, beach detours, or airport floor breaks.

- **Hack #299:** Mini First-Aid Stash

Band-aids, blister pads, ibuprofen, antihistamines. You don't need a full kit—just the essentials

- **Hack #300:** Face Mist + Hydration Combo

Pair a refreshing face mist with a big drink of water. It's like a brain and body wake-up.

Staying Grounded While Traveling

New places are exciting—but they can also throw off your rhythm. Travel can make you feel a little... floaty. These hacks are about helping you feel rooted, calm, and connected—no matter where you are.

Create small rituals, carry familiar comforts, and build in moments to pause. Grounded travelers are happy travelers.

- **Hack #301:** The Morning Anchor

Start your day with one familiar habit: journaling, stretching, or just sipping coffee slowly.

- **Hack #302:** Location Pin Drop

Drop a pin wherever you're staying. Getting lost? Open maps and tap back "home."

- **Hack #303:** The No-Rush Arrival Rule

When you get somewhere new, take 30 minutes to settle in. Unpack, breathe, look around. Then explore.

- **Hack #304:** Travel Totem Trick

Bring one small object from home—a stone, photo, or charm. It helps create continuity.

- **Hack #305:** Reflective Mini Journal

Capture one moment from each day in a tiny notebook. It helps you slow down and notice.

- **Hack #306:** Re-entry Buffer

When coming home, schedule a "nothing" day. Recharging before reality resumes is key.

Gear That Changes Everything

You don't need fancy luggage or high-tech gadgets, but a few clever pieces of gear can dramatically upgrade your travel game. The right tools = less stress, more ease.

Each item on this list has one job: make travel smoother, lighter, or more enjoyable. It's not just about where you're going—it's about feeling like yourself when you get there.

- **Hack #307:** The Folding Backpack

Carry a foldable daypack in your main bag. Perfect for day trips without hauling everything.

- **Hack #308:** The Cord Taco

Keep chargers and cables tidy with velcro wraps, cord tacos, or small zip pouches.

- **Hack #309:** Travel Power Strip

Hotels never have enough outlets. A small power strip or USB hub keeps everything charged.

- **Hack #310:** The Universal Adapter Hero

Get one with multiple USB ports. Bonus points if it has surge protection.

- **Hack #311:** Compression Bag Boost

Use vacuum-free compression bags to shrink clothes without needing tools. More space, same stuff.

- **Hack #312:** Travel Shoe Bags

Keep dirty soles away from clean clothes. Reusable, lightweight, and essential.

Staying Productive While Traveling

Being on the go doesn't mean pressing pause on your projects. Whether you're a freelancer, remote worker, or just like to use downtime wisely, these hacks help you stay sharp, without overloading your brain.

It's not about hustling every second. It's about smart momentum in the cracks of time. Because even a little focused progress can make a travel day feel surprisingly productive

- **Hack #313:** Pocket Goals List

Jot 1–3 simple goals each travel day. "Answer 3 emails." "Write 100 words." Small wins count.

- **Hack #314:** Work-from-Anywhere Setup

Keep a light laptop sleeve, a collapsible stand, and noise-canceling earbuds. You're ready to go anywhere.

- **Hack #315:** The 20-Minute Rule

Use short pockets of time (train rides, lounges) to tackle quick tasks. Set a timer and sprint.

- **Hack #316:** Offline Brain Dump

No Wi-Fi? No problem. Use downtime to journal, outline, and plan. Offline time = creative gold.

- **Hack #317:** The Focused Playlist

Curate a playlist just for travel work time. Your brain will click into gear when it hears it.

- **Hack #318:** Schedule Lightly

Don't cram. Leave gaps in your itinerary for flexibility—and to actually get stuff done without the rush.

Health & Wellness Hacks

Fit(ish), Happy, and Functioning

Let's be honest—wellness can feel like a full-time job. Smoothies, supplements, 10,000 steps, six forms of self-care... it's enough to make you want to nap instead. But taking care of your body and mind doesn't have to be overwhelming or expensive.

This chapter is packed with practical, low-effort ways to feel a little better, physically and mentally, even when life is messy. It's wellness for real life, not Instagram. No gym memberships, juice cleanses, or sunrise meditations required. Just smart little tweaks that meet you where you are and help you feel more energized, more grounded, and a lot more human.

Sneaky Ways to Move More Daily

You don't need a gym membership or a two-hour workout routine to get more movement into your day. You just need a little nudge to keep your body from fossilizing into your desk chair. Movement boosts energy, sharpens focus, and (bonus) keeps your joints from creaking like a haunted house.

These hacks help you trick yourself into moving more, without feeling like you're 'working out.' Because fitness doesn't have to mean sweat-drenched sessions or counting reps, sometimes it just means stretching while the kettle boils or dancing while folding laundry. Tiny moves, big difference.

- **Hack #319:** Commercial Break Moves

During TV time, do 10 squats, 10 jumping jacks, or stretch during ads.

- **Hack #320:** Walk and Talk

Take calls while walking. Pacing counts.

- **Hack #321:** Bathroom Break Bonus

Do 10 calf raises or wall push-ups after every trip to the restroom.

- **Hack #322:** The Far Parking Spot

Park farther away on purpose. Those extra steps add up.

- **Hack #323:** Refill = Reset

Use a small water bottle so you have to get up and refill more often.

- **Hack #324:** The 25/5 Move Rule

For every 25 minutes at your desk, do 5 minutes of movement (stairs, stretches, squats).

Hydration Hacks You'll Actually Remember

Water is the ultimate life upgrade—more energy, clearer skin, fewer headaches, better mood. And yet… we forget. Or we remember and still don't drink it.

These hacks make hydration easy, automatic, and dare we say, kind of fun. You don't need to chug gallons or carry a novelty-sized jug—just build small habits that actually stick. Because a well-hydrated brain is a sharper, calmer, and more focused one.

- **Hack #325:** The Morning Chug

Start your day with a full glass of water before anything else.

- **Hack #326:** Marked-Up Bottle

Use a water bottle with time-stamped goals or mark it with a Sharpie.

- **Hack #327:** Hydration Triggers

Pair drinking water with daily habits (e.g., before brushing your teeth or after checking emails).

- **Hack #328:** Add Flavor, Not Sugar

Infuse your water with lemon, cucumber, mint, or berries for a tasty twist.

- **Hack #329:** App Reminder Nudge

Use apps like Plant Nanny or Water Reminder to keep you sipping.

- **Hack #330:** The Elastic Band Trick

Start with four bands on your bottle. Each time you finish a refill, slide one off.

2-Minute Morning and Night Routines

No need for a 14-step ritual or sunrise yoga on the balcony. You can upgrade your day with just two minutes of intention, morning and night.

These mini routines help you start strong and wind down well, no pressure or perfection required. Because real-life routines need to be flexible, forgiving, and fast. A tiny dose of consistency can anchor your day more than any expensive wellness trend ever could.

- **Hack #331:** The Morning Stretch + Breathe

Two minutes of full-body stretch plus deep breathing = calm, awake body.

- **Hack #332:** Gratitude Quick List

Write down three things you're grateful for in the morning or before bed.

- **Hack #333:** Set Your One Thing

Choose one focus task for the day. Say it out loud. Own it.

- **Hack #334:** Nighttime Reset Timer

Set a 2-minute timer to tidy one surface before bed. It'll change your mornings.

- **Hack #335:** Face + Teeth Stack

Combine skincare and brushing teeth into a two-minute ritual. No skipping.

- **Hack #336:** Digital Wind-Down

Set your phone to grayscale or Do Not Disturb two minutes before bed.

Budget-Friendly Meal Prep

Healthy eating shouldn't cost a fortune or take all weekend. With a few smart shortcuts, you can prep like a pro, even if you hate cooking.

These hacks help you save money, reduce waste, and always have something decent to eat, without the stress. No fancy equipment, no color-coded containers—just real food, simple systems, and meals that won't make you dread your fridge.

- **Hack #337:** The Big Batch Base

Cook a giant base (rice, lentils, roasted veggies) and remix it all week.

- **Hack #338:** Mason Jar Salad Stack

Layer salad ingredients in jars. Dressing at the bottom, greens at the top.

- **Hack #339:** Theme Day Rotation

Pick easy weekly themes like Stir-Fry Monday or Soup Sunday to simplify shopping.

- **Hack #340:** Freeze It Flat

Store cooked meals in freezer bags laid flat. Saves space and defrosts faster.

- **Hack #341:** Grocery List Anchor

Always keep staples like eggs, oats, and frozen veggies on hand for no-brainer meals.

- **Hack #342:** The Leftovers Bin

Dedicate one fridge shelf to leftovers. Use it or lose it by Friday.

Life-Saving Posture Fixes

Posture problems aren't just about looking slouchy—they can cause headaches, back pain, and drain your energy. The good news? You don't need a posture brace or a chiropractor on speed dial to fix it.

These posture hacks are easy to do, don't take long, and will have you sitting (and standing) taller in no time. Because good posture isn't just about spine health—it affects your focus, your mood, and even how confident you feel in your own body.

- **Hack #343:** Chin Tuck Check

Several times a day, gently pull your chin back (like a double chin). Resets your spine.

- **Hack #344:** Sit on a Towel Roll

Placing a rolled-up towel behind your lower back supports your spine naturally.

- **Hack #345:** Screen Height Hack

Raise your laptop or monitor so the top third of the screen is eye level.

- **Hack #346:** Shoulder Blade Squeeze

Every hour, squeeze your shoulder blades together for 10 seconds.

- **Hack #347:** Alarm Stretch Stack

Set phone alarms to remind you to check posture and stretch every 90 minutes.

- **Hack #348:** Standing Desk Shifts

Even if you don't have a standing desk, use a box or shelf to mix sitting and standing.

How to Stretch Without Going to Yoga

Stretching is magic for your muscles, joints, and mood. But if you're not into classes or complicated poses, don't worry. These simple stretches fit into real life—no mat or mindfulness mantra required. You can sneak them in while waiting for the kettle to boil or during a Netflix binge. It's all about releasing tension and moving better, without rolling out a yoga mat in your living room.

- **Hack #349:** Doorway Chest Opener

Stand in a doorway, arms out at 90°, and lean gently forward. Instant chest release.

- **Hack #350:** Couch Hip Stretch

Put one leg on the couch, knee down, and gently lean forward. Hello, hip flexors.

- **Hack #351:** Desk Shoulder Roll

Shrug shoulders up to your ears, roll back, then drop. Repeat 5x every few hours.

- **Hack #352:** Seated Forward Fold

Sit on the floor, legs straight, and lean forward. Great for hamstrings and helps calm a racing mind.

- **Hack #353:** Wrist + Forearm Relief

Gently pull back each hand for a 10-second forearm stretch. Great for keyboard warriors.

- **Hack #354:** Calf Stretch Step

Stand on a step, heels off the edge, and lower down gently. Stretch and strengthen.

Cures, Fixes & Quick Solutions

Because You Don't Have Time to Google It

Let's face it—when something goes wrong, you don't always have time to fall down a rabbit hole of articles, product reviews, or contradictory advice. You need a fix, and you need it fast. Whether it's a stubborn headache, a smelly shoe situation, or a zipper that's decided to quit mid-commute, this chapter delivers simple, practical solutions without the information overload.

This isn't about being perfect. It's about being prepared. These bite-sized hacks are here to rescue you from life's random curveballs—from surprise stains to mysterious bloating to that one screw that won't come loose. Quick, useful, and real-world tested—because Googling shouldn't be your emergency plan.

Quick Fixes for Headaches, Stains & Sore Throats

Head pounding, shirt stained, or throat tickling? You don't have time to scroll through twelve articles full of pop-ups and home remedy debates. You need answers. Fast.

These hacks skip the fluff and go straight to action. Whether it's a midday migraine, a coffee spill before your big meeting, or a sore throat creeping in at 10 PM, here's what actually helps.

- **Hack #355:** The Cold + Caffeine Combo

For tension headaches, press a cold pack on your neck and sip a small coffee. The combo helps shrink blood vessels and ease the pain.

- **Hack #356:** The Pencil Trick

Hold a pencil between your teeth (don't bite). It relaxes jaw tension that can trigger headaches.

- **Hack #357:** Club Soda Stain Zap

Blot the stain, pour club soda over it, and blot again. It works wonders on wine, coffee, and mystery lunch spots.

- **Hack #358:** Salt Water Soothe

Gargle warm salt water for 30 seconds to calm a sore throat. Do it a few times a day.

- **Hack #359:** Honey + Lemon Shot

Mix 1 tbsp of honey with lemon juice and warm water. Instant throat relief—no cough syrup needed.

- **Hack #360:** Shirt Saver Hack

No stain remover? Rub a bit of dish soap into the stain, let it sit for 5 minutes, then rinse. It's gentle and effective.

Sleep, Breath & Bloating: Your Body's Weird SOS Signals

You're exhausted but can't sleep. You feel fine, but smell like a breath mint commercial gone wrong. Or you're bloated like you swallowed a balloon. Welcome to the weird but fixable side of being human.

These low-effort solutions tackle body issues that mess with your day—or your night—without needing a doctor or a 3-step detox.

- **Hack #361:** The 4-7-8 Sleep Trick

Inhale for 4 seconds, hold for 7, exhale for 8. Repeat. It slows your heart rate and signals your body to chill.

- **Hack #362:** Pillow Scent Reset

Spritz your pillow with lavender spray before bed. It's calming, and smells like you've got your life together.

- **Hack #363:** Apple for Breath

Crunchy apples help scrub your teeth and neutralize breath—way better than gum if you're stuck without a brush.

- **Hack #364:** Baking Soda Rinse

Mix 1 tsp of baking soda in a glass of water. Gargle to fight bad breath. Swish, spit, repeat.

- **Hack #365:** Ginger Chew for Bloat

Chew on a small piece of ginger or pop a ginger chew after meals. It eases digestion and deflates the belly bloat.

- **Hack #366:** The Belly Massage

Gently massage your stomach clockwise to move gas along. Works especially well after flying or eating too fast.

- **Hack #367:** Light Dinner Rule

Heavy late-night meals = restless sleep. Stick to something light and stop eating 2 hours before bed.

Fix a Stuck Zipper, Flat Pillow, or Funky Shoes

Life is too short for broken zippers, pancake pillows, and shoes that smell like regret. These everyday annoyances show up uninvited and tend to strike at the worst possible moments—right before a meeting, a night out, or when you're already running late.

The good news? You don't need a toolkit, a DIY YouTube marathon, or a perfectly curated Pinterest board to fix them. Just a few clever tricks, common household items, and a little know-how can get things back in working order—fast. Time saved, stress dodged, dignity intact.

- **Hack #368:** Pencil Zipper Rescue

Rub graphite from a regular pencil on the teeth of a stuck zipper. Wiggle it loose. Repeat as needed.

- **Hack #369:** Pillow Fluff Revival

Toss your sad, flat pillow in the dryer with a tennis ball for 10 minutes. Hello, loft.

- **Hack #370:** The Shoe Shakeout

Got sand, pebbles, or whatever lurking inside your shoes? Use a hair dryer on cool to blast them out.

- **Hack #371:** Dryer Sheet Stuffers

Pop dryer sheets into smelly shoes overnight. Removes stink without soaking anything.

- **Hack #372:** The Steam Refresh

Hold wrinkled clothes near the shower steam while you wash. Instant de-wrinkling with zero ironing.

- **Hack #373:** Lint Roller Rescue

Use a lint roller to clean lampshades, drawer interiors, and pet-hair-covered everything.

Instant Shoe Deodorizers & Smell Hacks

You love your sneakers. Your nose... not so much. Shoe odor is one of those sneaky problems that slowly creeps up until it ambushes you—and anyone nearby. It's stubborn, awkward, and weirdly personal.

But the fix doesn't have to be complicated or expensive. These hacks are simple, quick, and effective—most can be done while brushing your teeth or brewing coffee. Because your kicks should turn heads, not wrinkle noses.

- **Hack #374:** Tea Bag Fresheners

Drop two dry black tea bags in each shoe overnight. The tannins fight bacteria and soak up smells.

- **Hack #375:** Baking Soda Bomb

Pour 1-2 tablespoons of baking soda into each shoe, shake, and leave overnight. Dump it out in the morning.

- **Hack #376:** Essential Oil Boost

Add a drop of tea tree or lavender oil to a cotton ball. Toss it in your shoes for all-natural odor control.

- **Hack #377:** Freezer Trick

Pop shoes in a plastic bag and freeze overnight. Cold kills bacteria = no more funk.

- **Hack #378:** Citrus Peel Pockets

Place lemon or orange peels inside your shoes overnight. It absorbs odors and leaves a zesty scent behind.

Vinegar: The Unsung Hero of Home Remedies

Vinegar isn't just for salads—it's basically a miracle fluid in disguise. It cleans, deodorizes, disinfects, detangles, dissolves, and even soothes. If there were a Swiss Army knife in liquid form, it would be this stuff. Cheap, natural, and already sitting in your pantry.

Here's how to unleash its full, sour-scented power—from cleaning hacks to quick fixes that make you wonder why you didn't start using it sooner.

- **Hack #379:** Deodorant Stain Fix

Spray white vinegar on armpit stains before washing. Say goodbye to crusty t-shirts.

- **Hack #380:** Showerhead Descaler

Tie a bag of vinegar around your showerhead and leave overnight. Removes buildup, boosts pressure.

- **Hack #381:** Bug Bite Itch Stopper

Dab apple cider vinegar on itchy bites. Cools and relieves fast.

- **Hack #382:** Drain Deodorizer

Pour ½ cup vinegar + ½ cup baking soda down your drain. Wait 10 minutes, then rinse with hot water.

- **Hack #383:** Glass Cleaner

Mix equal parts vinegar and water in a spray bottle = streak-free windows, mirrors, and screens.

- **Hack #384:** Sore Muscle Soak

Add 1-2 cups of apple cider vinegar to a warm bath. It helps ease tension and soothe sore spots.

DIY or Call the Pro? (Spoiler: Not Everything Needs You)

Some problems need duct tape and determination. Others need someone with a van, a toolkit, and liability insurance. The line between "I've got this" and "I should really call someone" isn't always obvious—until you're ankle-deep in water or halfway into dismantling your washing machine.

Here's how to tell when you can MacGyver it with confidence—and when it's time to step back and let the pros take the wheel (before things get worse).

- **Hack #385:** The Rule of Three

Try three things to fix it. If it's not solved, stop. You're either wasting time or making it worse.

- **Hack #386:** The Time Cost Test

Ask: Would it take a pro 10 minutes and me 2 hours? Book the pro.

- **Hack #387:** YouTube First Stop

Check YouTube. If a fix has fewer than 3 steps and you have the tools, you're good to go.

- **Hack #388:** Red Flag Repairs

Call a pro for anything electrical, gas-related, or that leaks near your ceiling. Don't risk it.

- **Hack #389:** Skill-for-Hire Swap

Trade skills with a friend. You fix their spreadsheet, they fix your leaky tap. Everyone wins.

- **Hack #390:** Emergency List on Hand

Keep a short list of go-to repair contacts in your phone. When stuff breaks, you don't have to Google in panic mode.

Emergency Cleanups & Spill Saves

Some messes can't wait. Spilled wine, gum on your jeans, or candle wax melted into the carpet—these little disasters hit fast and demand immediate damage control. And let's be honest, the longer you stall, the harder they are to fix.

These cleanup hacks are built for speed and sanity. No panic, no fancy tools, and definitely no Pinterest perfectionism—just practical, grab-what-you've-got fixes that actually work when you're in the middle of a mess.

- **Hack #391:** Wax Paper Spill Trick

Use a credit card and wax paper to gently lift candle wax from fabric. Then place paper towels above and below and iron on low to pull out the rest.

- **Hack #392:** Salt on Red Wine

Blot the spill, then cover with salt. Let it absorb the wine, then vacuum or brush off. It lifts a shocking amount.

- **Hack #393:** Ice Cube Gum Hack

Press an ice cube on the stuck gum to harden it. Once stiff, gently scrape off with a spoon or butter knife.

- **Hack #394:** Grease Stain Fix

Rub chalk or baking soda into a fresh grease spot. Let sit for 15 mins, then brush off and launder.

- **Hack #395:** Shaving Cream Carpet Saver

Apply white foam shaving cream to carpet stains. Let it sit for 5 mins, blot, and rinse. It works on everything from coffee to pet mess.

Burn, Bite, or Splinter? Fix It Fast

Minor injuries have a talent for showing up at the worst times—burns from baking, bug bites from just trying to enjoy the outdoors, or that splinter you picked up from who knows where. They're small, annoying, and often more disruptive than they have any right to be.

These are the quick, calm-down hacks you need in the moment. No first-aid kit? No problem. With a few everyday items and the right know-how, you can soothe the sting, skip the stress, and get back to living your life.

- **Hack #396:** Spoon Trick

Heat a metal spoon under hot water (not too hot!), then press it onto the bite for 10–20 seconds. It can neutralize the proteins in the saliva that cause itching.

- **Hack #397:** Aloe Ice Cubes

Freeze aloe vera in an ice tray. Perfect for instant relief from burns, bites, and sun-overdose skin.

- **Hack #398:** Baking Soda Bee Relief

Make a paste of baking soda and water and dab it on a bee sting or mosquito bite. It calms the itch and reduces swelling.

- **Hack #399:** Sugar-Soap Splinter Trick

No tweezers? No problem. Mix a little sugar and dish soap into a paste, smear it on a plaster, and stick it over the splinter. Leave it on overnight. The combo softens the skin and can help draw the splinter out gently..

- **Hack #400:** Cold Spoon on Burn

Place a cold metal spoon directly onto a minor burn. It pulls heat out quickly and calms the pain.

- **Hack #401:** Apple Cider Vinegar Dab

Dab a little ACV on itchy bug bites. It stings for a second, but takes the itch down fast.

Fashion Malfunctions Fixed Fast

Zippers break, buttons pop, deodorant streaks appear, and static cling attacks with zero warning—usually right when you're walking out the door or already five minutes late. Wardrobe malfunctions don't care about your schedule.

These hacks are your style-saving backup plan. Quick, clever, and completely doable in a bathroom stall or the backseat of an Uber—they'll keep your outfit together (literally) and help you show up looking like nothing ever happened.

- **Hack #402:** Clear Nail Polish Saver

Dab clear polish on a loose button thread to keep it from unraveling mid-way.

- **Hack #403:** Deodorant Streak Eraser

Rub a clean, dry fabric or dryer sheet over white marks to make them disappear. No water needed.

- **Hack #404:** Razor for Pills

Gently shave sweater pills with a clean, disposable razor. It freshens up knits fast.

- **Hack #405:** Static Sheet Swipe

Rub a dryer sheet across your clothes to kill static cling. Works great on skirts and tights.

- **Hack #406:** Double-Sided Tape Fix

Stick some double-sided tape inside your blouse or wrap dress to prevent gaping or slipping.

Kitchen Crises You Can Actually Fix

Burnt pans, stuck lids, and mystery fridge smells—kitchen chaos doesn't discriminate. Whether you're a confident cook or just trying not to burn toast, these little disasters sneak in fast and threaten to derail your entire dinner.

But don't panic. These quick-fix kitchen hacks are here to save your cookware, your sanity, and your meal. No meltdown, no last-minute grocery run, and no emergency takeout order required—just smart, simple solutions that actually work.

- **Hack #407:** Burnt Pan Rescue

Fill the pan with water and dish soap. Bring to a boil for 5 minutes, then scrub. Most gunk wipes right off.

- **Hack #408:** Bread for Broken Glass

Use a slice of bread to gently press over the floor where the glass shattered. It picks up tiny shards that your eyes miss.

- **Hack #409:** Wilted Greens Revival

Soak limp herbs or greens in cold water with a few ice cubes. In 10 minutes, they perk right up.

- **Hack #410:** Rubber Band Lid Trick

Wrap a thick rubber band around a stubborn jar lid. Instant grip without breaking a sweat.

- **Hack #411:** Microwave Reset

Heat a bowl of water with lemon slices for 3 minutes. Let it steam, then wipe the microwave clean with one swipe.

Fix-It Hacks for Your Car, Bag, or Desk

Your everyday carry items—car, bag, desk—have one job: make life easier. But it's chaos when zippers jam or chargers vanish into the void.

These clever fixes keep your essentials functional, organized, and (almost) stress-free.

- **Hack #412:** Binder Clip Cable Keeper

Clip one to the edge of your desk. Thread your charging cables through the metal arms to keep them from disappearing forever.

- **Hack #413:** Hand Sanitizer Lock De-Icer

If your car door lock freezes, dab hand sanitizer (alcohol-based) on your key. It melts ice fast.

- **Hack #414:** Sunglasses Case Survival Kit

Use an old case to store gum, earbuds, chargers, or emergency snacks. Toss it in your bag and go.

- **Hack #415:** Nail File Zipper Fix

Use a nail file to smooth out zipper teeth or clean grime that's making it stick.

- **Hack #416:** Velcro Charger Mount

Stick a square of Velcro under your desk or in your car. Wrap the other piece around your charger. Boom—no more digging.

Survival & Safety Hacks

MacGyver Your Way Through It

You don't have to be a wilderness survivalist or doomsday prepper to benefit from a few good safety hacks. Emergencies happen—power goes out, phones vanish, plans collapse—and when they do, a tiny bit of prep makes a huge difference.

This chapter is about everyday survival: what to do when the lights go out, your keys are locked in your car, or a storm reroutes your life. It's not about panic. It's about calm, quick action and simple strategies that help you move through the chaos with confidence.

What to Do in a Car Emergency

You're on the road, your car sputters, and suddenly, you're stranded. It's not just annoying. It can be dangerous, disorienting, and stressful, especially if you're alone or somewhere unfamiliar. And of course, it never happens on a warm sunny afternoon with full signal and snacks.

The trick? Stay visible, stay calm, and know your basics. These hacks help you handle roadside surprises like dead batteries, weird noises, and flat tires without spiraling into full panic mode. Just a little prep goes a long way when you're stuck in the park.

- **Hack #417:** Pull Over Smart

Move safely off the road—preferably to a flat, visible area. Turn on your hazard lights immediately.

- **Hack #418:** Window Signal Hack

Hang a plastic bag, tissue, or piece of cloth from your window to signal you need help.

- **Hack #419:** Glovebox Go-Tos

Keep a small kit in your glovebox: flashlight, phone charger, emergency cash, bandages, and a whistle or safety cutter.

- **Hack #420:** Tire Check Reminder

Set a calendar alert every 2 months to check your tire pressure (including your spare). It takes 5 minutes and saves a world of stress.

- **Hack #421:** Paper Map Backup

Keep a basic map of your region in the car. GPS fails—paper doesn't.

What to Do During a Power Outage

The lights go out, your phone's dying, and your fridge is now a ticking clock. Power outages can feel disorienting and weirdly isolating, especially when you realize how much you rely on electricity for comfort, safety, and entertainment.

But a little prep can turn lights-off chaos into a surprisingly calm (maybe even cozy) situation. These hacks help you stay calm, connected, and a step ahead—whether it's a short flicker or a full evening in the dark.

- **Hack #422:** Flashlight in Every Room

Stash small flashlights or tap lights in drawers, nightstands, or near the door. The more accessible, the better.

- **Hack #423:** Phone on Low Power

Switch your phone to low-power mode and dim the screen to stretch every last percent.

- **Hack #424:** Fridge Hack = Tape Trick

Place a piece of tape on a cup of ice in your freezer. If it melts and refreezes, you'll know your food thawed (and might be unsafe).

- **Hack #425:** Solar Light Trick

Recharge solar garden lights during the day and bring them inside at night for soft, free lighting.

- **Hack #426:** Nearest Power Pit Stop

Know the nearest coffee shop, library, or friend's house with power in case of long outages.

What to Do If You Lose Your Phone

Losing your phone is like misplacing your brain, wallet, and entire social life all at once. It's a modern-day crisis that hits hard, especially when you realize how much you rely on that little device for everything from directions to payments to emergency contacts.

But don't panic. Act fast, stay focused, and use these hacks to lock things down or, if you're lucky, get your phone back. These are your digital lifelines when your tech suddenly goes MIA.

- **Hack #427:** "Find My" Setup Check

Make sure your phone has location tracking enabled (like Find My iPhone or Find My Device for Android). Test it once—it takes two minutes.

- **Hack #428:** Lock Screen Backup Info

Set your lock screen with an alternate contact—email or a friend's number—so a kind stranger can reach you.

- **Hack #429:** Location History Option

Use your Google or Apple account's location history to trace where your phone's been.

- **Hack #430:** Remote Wipe Ready

Know how to remotely lock or erase your phone. It's better to lose data than risk identity theft.

- **Hack #431:** Contact Access System

Make sure you've got your key contacts stored somewhere else, too—like your computer, paper card, or cloud drive.

Fire, Flood, and Lockout Hacks

Natural disasters and everyday disasters don't show up politely. A fire alarm starts blaring, water creeps into the hallway, or you find yourself locked out—barefoot, in pajamas, holding a lukewarm coffee. These aren't wild hypotheticals. They're real-life curveballs that hit fast and without warning.

The goal isn't to avoid every crisis—it's to move smarter when they happen. These hacks help you stay calm, buy time, and create safe exits when the unexpected knocks (or kicks) the door down.

- **Hack #432:** Exit Drill Lite

Know two exits from every room in your house—even if it means through a window. Practice once a year.

- **Hack #433:** The Wet Towel Trick

In a smoky environment, place a damp towel at the base of a door to block smoke from coming through.

- **Hack #434:** Stuck Door Flood Escape

If water pressure keeps the door shut, break a window with a seatbelt or removable headrest bar.

- **Hack #435:** Lockout Lifeline

Keep a copy of your key with a trusted neighbor or in a combo lockbox outside your home.

- **Hack #436:** Fire-Safe Folder

Store copies of IDs, insurance docs, and emergency cash in a waterproof, fire-resistant folder you can grab fast.

- **Hack #437:** Code Word System

Create a "safe word" to use with kids or roommates in emergencies for fast, silent communication.

Backup Contacts and Emergency Cards

In a phone-obsessed world, most of us can't even recite our best friend's number, let alone our doctor's or emergency contact. But when your phone is dead, stolen, or doing the backstroke in a puddle, those numbers become everything.

This section is about creating a backup plan for your digital life. These simple hacks make sure you're never truly disconnected—even when your phone is. Let's make sure you're not stuck without a lifeline.

- **Hack #438:** Wallet Card Essentials

Write down 2–3 emergency contacts, allergies, and any medications. Keep it in your wallet or purse.

- **Hack #439:** ICE Your Phone

Add "ICE" (In Case of Emergency) before your top contact names so first responders know who to call.

- **Hack #440:** Family Contact Sheet

Stick a printed contact sheet on your fridge or by the door. Great for babysitters or neighbors.

- **Hack #441:** Screenshot Your Life

Take screenshots of your ID, insurance, and medical info and store them in a secure photo album.

- **Hack #442:** Cloud Save Backup

Use a secure app like LastPass, Notion, or Google Drive to store emergency docs, passwords, and contacts.

- **Hack #443:** Number Tattoo (Just Kidding... Sort of)

If you're traveling solo, keep emergency numbers in more than one place—wallet, luggage tag, and even written on paper tucked in your shoe.

Creating a "Go Bag" for Adults

A "go bag" isn't just for doomsday preppers or zombie apocalypses. It's for real-life moments—power outages, last-minute evacuations, burst pipes, or that one time you needed to crash somewhere unexpectedly and had nothing but your phone charger and hope.

The point isn't perfection—it's preparedness. Your go bag doesn't have to be fancy. It just needs to be packed with the essentials so you can grab it, go, and handle whatever chaos is waiting outside the door.

- **Hack #444:** Essentials First

Pack copies of IDs, cash, a phone charger, flashlight, snacks, water, and basic meds in a small backpack or tote.

- **Hack #445:** Clothes that Work

Include one change of clothes, socks, and a hoodie. Go for neutral, layerable, and clean.

- **Hack #446:** Power Bank = Lifeline

Always keep a charged power bank in your go bag. Check it monthly.

- **Hack #447:** Pet Prep Add-On

Got a furry sidekick? Add a collapsible bowl, some kibble, a leash, and a copy of vet records.

- **Hack #448:** Expiry Check Calendar

Set a calendar reminder every 6 months to check your go bag's food, batteries, and meds.

- **Hack #449:** Add a Calm Kit

A notebook, small puzzle, book, or headphones can calm your nerves in tense situations.

Life-Saving Habits (Know Your Exits, Know Your Meds)

Big emergencies are (thankfully) rare. But it's the little daily habits that quietly stack up to save lives when things go sideways. Knowing your exits, having your meds list handy, or grabbing your flashlight without thinking—those aren't just details. They're what help you stay safe when seconds count.

It's not about being paranoid or living on edge. It's about being quietly, confidently ready for whatever life throws your way.

- **Hack #450:** Exit Awareness Rule

In public places (malls, hotels, theaters), clock the exits. Just a glance, every time.

- **Hack #451:** Med Card Mini

Keep a small list of current meds, dosages, and allergies in your wallet or on your phone.

- **Hack #452:** Shoe Rule for Sleepers

Keep your shoes by the bed. In an emergency, the last thing you want is bare feet and broken glass.

- **Hack #453:** Flashlight Habit Loop

Put a flashlight or headlamp by your bed and teach yourself to grab it when the lights flicker.

- **Hack #454:** What-If Mapping

Once a month, pick one "what if?" scenario (power outage, fire, car breakdown) and mentally walk through how you'd handle it.

- **Hack #455:** Teach Someone Else

Share one of your new safety habits with a friend, kid, or partner. Bonus: you'll remember it better, too.

Money & Budget Hacks

Save Without Suffering

Saving money doesn't have to mean sacrificing everything you love. You don't have to cut out all takeout, cancel every subscription, or start couponing like it's a competitive sport. Small, smart shifts can stretch your cash further, without making your life miserable in the process.

This chapter is all about those little tweaks that add up. We'll cover smarter ways to spend, stash, and simplify. Whether you're trying to get out of debt, build a buffer, or just make your money go a little further each month, these hacks will help you feel in control, without the budget guilt spiral.

Automate Your Savings

Willpower is unreliable. Motivation comes and goes. But systems? Systems don't forget to transfer R500 into your savings, even when you're tired, busy, or just not thinking about it. Automating your money is one of the easiest, most effective ways to build financial habits that actually stick—because you're not relying on daily discipline.

Set it once, and it runs quietly in the background while you live your life. These hacks help you save painlessly and consistently, without thinking about it every month.

- **Hack #456:** The Pay-Yourself-First Transfer

Set up a recurring transfer that moves money to savings as soon as your income hits. Out of sight, into your safety net.

- **Hack #457:** The Round-Up Booster

Use banking tools or apps that round up your purchases and save the spare change. It adds up without effort.

- **Hack #458:** The Hidden Savings Account

Open a separate savings account with a boring name (e.g., "Do Not Touch"). Out of sight = out of temptation.

- **Hack #459:** The 52-Week Ladder

Start with saving $10 the first week, then increase by $10 each week. By the end of the year? $13,780 saved.

- **Hack #460:** The Payday Split

Instead of one big paycheck, split part of it into categories like "fun," "bills," and "future you." Gives every dollar a job.

"No-Spend" Challenge Tips

No-spend challenges sound intense—but they're surprisingly freeing. Think of it like a detox for your wallet. You temporarily cut out the extras, reset your habits, and get creative with what you already have. It's less about restriction and more about awareness—learning where your money goes and what actually adds value.

The goal isn't to suffer—it's to gain clarity. These hacks help you survive (and maybe even enjoy) a no-spend challenge without losing your mind, your momentum, or your social life.

- **Hack #461:** Define Your Rules

Choose your category: no dining out? No clothing? No impulse buys? Clear rules = fewer excuses.

- **Hack #462:** Pick a Timeframe

Start small. Try a weekend, a week, or one paycheck cycle. Then stretch it if it's working.

- **Hack #463:** Create a Fun-Free List

Make a go-to list of fun things that cost zero. Picnics, game nights, closet decluttering with a friend—it all counts.

- **Hack #464:** Visualize Your "Why"

Print a picture of what you're saving for (debt-free living? a trip? emergency cushion?) and stick it to your fridge or wallet.

- **Hack #465:** Budget a Cheat Pass

Allow one small exception per week (like a coffee or takeaway snack). Keeps you sane while still sticking to your goal.

- **Hack #466:** Track Your Wins

Each time you say "no" to a purchase, write down the amount you saved. Watch that motivation grow.

Grocery Gameplan to Cut Your Bill

Food is one of the biggest flexible expenses in most budgets, and also one of the sneakiest ways money slips through the cracks. A few extra impulse snacks, a forgotten ingredient, or midweek takeout can add up fast. The secret? Plan like a minimalist, shop like a boss, and never hit the store hungry.

You don't need to coupon obsessively or survive on instant noodles. These hacks help you cut your grocery bill while still eating well, wasting less, and keeping your sanity intact.

- **Hack #467:** Meal Plan Before You Shop

Decide on 3–5 dinners for the week. Make a list of those meals. Stick to it.

- **Hack #468:** Shop Your Kitchen First

Before writing your list, look in your fridge, freezer, and pantry. Use up what's already there.

- **Hack #469:** Use the "One-More-Day" Rule

Stretch your groceries by just one more day before restocking. Eat leftovers or get creative.

- **Hack #470:** Stick to the Outer Aisles

Fresh food, bulk staples, and fewer distractions live on the perimeter. Most overspending happens in the middle.

- **Hack #471:** Try Generic First

Buy store brands for staples like pasta, canned goods, and rice. If you hate it, switch back next time.

- **Hack #472:** Pick One "Treat" Per Shop

Give yourself one fun item (chocolate, fancy coffee, a frozen dessert). Keeps things satisfying—without a full-on splurge.

Smart Digital Subscriptions Cleanup

Streaming, cloud storage, apps, delivery services... it all adds up faster than you realize. What starts as "just R99/month" quietly snowballs into hundreds over the year, often for things you forgot you subscribed to or barely use anymore.

The goal isn't to cancel everything—it's to keep what you love and ditch what's draining your wallet. These hacks help you trim the digital fat, simplify your tech life, and make space (and money) for what actually matters.

- **Hack #473:** Run a Sub Check

Go through your app store, bank statement, or email inbox. List out every active subscription.

- **Hack #474:** Use the "Cancel & Wait" Rule

Cancel a subscription, but don't replace it right away. If you miss it in 30 days, consider reactivating.

- **Hack #475:** Share Where You Can

Split subscriptions (like Netflix, Spotify, Dropbox) with trusted family or friends if terms allow it.

- **Hack #476:** Bundle Smarter

Many services offer discounted bundles (e.g., streaming + music + storage). Look for overlap and consolidate.

- **Hack #477:** Swap for Free Alternatives

There are amazing free tools for everything—streaming, budgeting, workouts, and cloud storage. You just have to look.

- **Hack #478:** Set Subscription Reminders

Use your calendar to alert you one week before renewal dates. Gives you time to cancel before getting charged.

Hacks for Second-hand Deals

Why buy new when secondhand can be better—and way cheaper? Preloved items often cost a fraction of the original price, come with personality, and skip the wasteful packaging. Whether you're thrifting in person, swapping with friends, or scrolling Facebook Marketplace at midnight, the savings are real—and sometimes surprising.

These hacks help you score quality finds, avoid common pitfalls, and stretch your budget further, without sacrificing style, function, or fun.

- **Hack #479:** Know Your Must-Haves

Make a wishlist of high-quality items worth buying secondhand—kitchen gear, tools, furniture, books, clothes, etc.

- **Hack #480:** Time Your Thrift Runs

Go mid-week for the best inventory. By the weekend, the best finds are often long gone.

- **Hack #481:** Always Ask for a Lower Price

On peer-to-peer sites, people expect you to negotiate. Be polite and direct. You'll save more often than not.

- **Hack #482:** Check the "Free" Listings

Many platforms have a free section where people just want stuff gone. Set alerts for big-ticket items.

- **Hack #483:** Create a Clothing Swap Group

Coordinate with friends or neighbors to exchange clothes, kids' gear, or accessories. Everyone wins.

- **Hack #484:** Think "Refurb," Not "New"

Tech, appliances, and tools can often be bought certified refurbished—cheaper, tested, and usually with a warranty.

Receipt Hacks for Instant Wins

Receipts are boring—but they're also loaded with hidden wins. From price adjustments and cashback offers to spotting overcharges, that crumpled piece of paper (or emailed version) is more valuable than it looks. Tracking your receipts is a small habit that can deliver surprisingly big returns.

These hacks help you squeeze extra value from what you're already spending—without changing your lifestyle or adding more work to your plate.

- **Hack #491:** Snap & Save

Use apps like SnapnSave, Fetch Rewards, or Zapper to scan receipts and earn cashback or points.

- **Hack #492:** Refund Window Watch

If you see a price drop within a store's refund window (usually 7–14 days), go back and claim the difference.

- **Hack #493:** Scan for Duplicates

Check receipts for double-charged items or small pricing errors. It happens more often than you'd think.

- **Hack #494:** Keep Big-Ticket Receipts Together

Put warranties, returns, or insurance claims, store appliance and electronics receipts in a labeled folder or photo album.

- **Hack #495:** Track Spending Patterns

Toss them into a jar or folder and do a once-a-month review. Patterns = power.

Low-Budget Learning & Growth

Self-improvement doesn't have to be expensive. In fact, most of what you want to learn is already out there—free, accessible, and waiting for you to tap in. You don't need a pricey course or a fancy certification to grow. You just need curiosity and the right starting point.

These hacks help you level up your skills, expand your knowledge, and boost your confidence—without spending a cent or adding pressure to "do it all." Learn at your own pace, on your own terms.

- **Hack #496:** Join Your Local Library

Free books, audiobooks, streaming, courses, study spaces—you'd be surprised what your library offers.

- **Hack #497:** YouTube University

Learn anything from coding to painting to plumbing. Create playlists of trusted creators for easy access.

- **Hack #498:** Online Courses, Free Edition

Check out platforms like Coursera, edX, and Alison for free courses on just about everything.

- **Hack #499:** Community Workshops

Look for free events at community centers, universities, or coworking spaces. Great for learning and networking.

- **Hack #500:** Swap Skills with a Friend

Barter knowledge—teach a friend something you know in exchange for something they do. No money needed.

Laundry, Cleaning & Utility Savings

Your home eats money in subtle, sneaky ways—water trickling, lights left on, laundry running on high heat, and appliances silently sipping electricity. It all adds up, quietly raising your bills without much to show for it. But a few small tweaks? Total game-changers.

These hacks help you stretch your household budget by making your everyday routines more efficient, without sacrificing comfort, cleanliness, or your sanity.

- **Hack #501:** Cold Wash Everything

Cold water works just as well for most loads and saves on electricity.

- **Hack #502:** Air Dry What You Can

Cut your dryer time in half by hanging towels, sheets, and delicates.

- **Hack #503:** Off-Peak Power Hours

Check if your area has off-peak rates. Do laundry, charge devices, or run the dishwasher during those hours.

- **Hack #504:** DIY Cleaners

Use vinegar, lemon, and bicarb for effective, low-cost cleaning. Bonus: fewer chemicals.

- **Hack #505:** "One-Light" Rule

Challenge yourself to keep just one light on per room at night. It adds up.

Budgeting for Joy

Being smart with your money doesn't mean cutting out all the fun. In fact, building joy into your budget is what keeps you from burning out or feeling deprived. It's the little treats, spontaneous outings, and feel-good splurges that make life enjoyable—and help you stay committed to your bigger financial goals.

These hacks help you plan for pleasure without guilt, enjoy the moment, and still stay on track with your money. Because saving doesn't mean suffering.

- **Hack #506:** Create a "Fun Fund"

Set aside a small amount each month just for things you enjoy—no judgment, no guilt.

- **Hack #507:** Plan Your Splurges

Want to buy something pricey? Set a date, save in small amounts, and enjoy it fully when the time comes.

- **Hack #508:** Celebrate Cheaply

Host a potluck instead of dinner out, do DIY gifts, or create experience-based celebrations. Joy > cost.

- **Hack #509:** Use Free Trials Intentionally

Need a boost? Sign up for free classes, streaming services, or meal kits—but set a calendar reminder to cancel.

- **Hack #510:** Budget for Spontaneity

Leave 5–10% of your spending flexible. That way, saying "yes" to ice cream or a spontaneous concert won't derail your budget.

Conclusion & Bonus Tips
"Your Shortcut Starter Pack"

You made it to the end—but let's be honest, this isn't really the end. This is the *starting point* for hacking your day-to-day life with a little less chaos and a lot more ease.

You now have a toolkit packed with practical, realistic shortcuts—from taming your inbox to surviving a power outage to finally fixing that zipper without spiraling into a DIY meltdown. These aren't hacks for an imaginary life where everything goes to plan. These are for *your* life—the messy, beautiful, sometimes totally bonkers version where your phone dies, dinner burns, and your brain decides 3 am is the perfect time to relive that one awkward thing you said in 2015.

And here's the thing: you're not lazy. You're not disorganized. You're not bad at adulting. You're just doing the best you can in a world that doesn't always make it easy. And now? You're doing it *smarter*. The goal has never been perfection—it's been progress. Sustainable, doable, repeatable progress that fits into your real schedule and actual energy levels.

Whether you took notes, scribbled in the margins, dog-eared pages (respect), or just skimmed the parts you needed, every small change adds up. You don't need to do it all. You just need to do *one thing better* than yesterday. That's what hacking your life is really about.

Bonus: 10 Real Hacks from Real Humans

We reached out to readers, testers, and real-life life-hackers (a.k.a. everyday people like you) to share the clever things they swear by. Here are some of their favorites—low-effort, high-payoff, and 100% field-tested:

- "I set my kettle to boil while brushing my teeth in the morning—two birds, one stone."– *Lisa, 34, multitasker-in-chief*

- "My 'go bag' includes chocolate. Emergency or not, chocolate helps."– *Kay, 41, realist and snack survivalist*

- "I keep an empty laundry basket in my car for groceries. No more juggling oranges and oat milk."– *Sam, 27, logistics genius*

- "Post-it on the door: 'Phone, Wallet, Keys, Brain.' Haven't left anything behind since."– *Josh, 36, recovering forgetter*

- "I have a 'fridge first' bin labeled 'Eat Me First'—my produce waste dropped by half."– *Jess, 39, food waste warrior*

- "Every time I get a refund, I transfer it straight into savings. Out of sight, into stash."– *Mo, 30, stealth saver*

- "The Pomodoro method with music playlists changed how I work. I focus better and feel less tired."– *Ali, 29, remote worker extraordinaire*

- "Instead of buying new, I swap clothes with a friend twice a year. Free wardrobe refresh!"– *Nina, 43, style on a budget*

- "I have a voice note thread with myself. Every time I get an idea, I record it. Game changer."– *Reza, 38, creative brain wrangler*

- "Sunday night fridge clear-out + meal plan = no more mystery containers."– *Thabo, 35, reformed fridge archaeologist*

Keep Hacking Forward

You've got this. Not because you suddenly became someone else, but because you learned how to work smarter with the life you already have. These pages were never about becoming a perfectly optimized machine—they're about unlocking the version of you that feels a little more in control, a little less frazzled, and a lot more free.

Every time you grab a shortcut, rethink a routine, or solve a problem in under 60 seconds, you're proving one thing: life doesn't have to be harder than it already is. You can be clever without being complicated. You can be resourceful without being overwhelmed.

So here's your unofficial permission slip to keep experimenting. Try one new hack this week. Share your favorite with a friend. Make your own tweaks. Hack your life, your way.

And remember—life doesn't need a full reset. It just needs a few better shortcuts.

Thanks for showing up for yourself.

www.ingramcontent.com/pod-product-compliance
Lightning Source LLC
Chambersburg PA
CBHW052108070526
44584CB00017B/2384